The Young Entrepreneur's Playbook

"The journey of entrepreneurship is littered with twists and turns for every moment of success or failure. This playbook is a critical and purposeful guide for all aspiring entrepreneurs. It provides simple yet powerful concepts that will breathe life and meaning into every entrepreneur's unique journey. It also reminds one that nothing is impossible but with adequate preparation, sacrifice and consistency the entrepreneurs journey can be a resounding success."

IPELENG MKHARI, CEO MOTSENG INVESTMENTS

"These key lessons and insights in this all-important playbook are vital to fuel up every young entrepreneur on the journey to achieving greatness. Passion, perseverance and persistence, coupled with hard work, are the key ingredients of the world's most successful mega-entrepreneurs. Every morning before sunrise look at yourself in the mirror and repeat this: If I keep going and never give up, I will arrive at where I want to be."

MIKE ANDERSON, NSBC FOUNDER AND CEO

"Lindile Xoko has written a must-read book for anyone interested in uplifting the economy by starting and running a successful business as well as scaling it up to serve even more customers. The time for this book could not have been opportune as all types and sizes of businesses must rise from the chaos and devastation wreaked COVID-19 on economies around the world. This incisive and insightful book offers a treasure trove of useful and practical action steps a start-up business owner, or even the owner of a mature business, can take to ensure that it has a sound strategy, grow its customer base and serve its customers with class. The vast number of budding young entrepreneurs and those that have already embarked on their entrepreneurial journey will find this book a feast of ideas that they can use daily for themselves, their supporters, and teams to keep the business on track and growing. The author generously pours out pearls of wisdom garnered over many years of life and of being a business leader. Any serious entrepreneur wishing to start, grow a successful business and reap maximum benefits in the end should look no further than this playbook."

Dr Jerry Gule, CEO, Institute of People Management

The Young Entrepreneur's Playbook

Using Failure as a Shortcut to Success

Lindile Xoko

For my son, Qhawe Xavier Lindile Jr,
and my wife, Mihlali Xoko

First published by Jacana Media (Pty) Ltd in 2021

10 Orange Street
Sunnyside
Auckland Park 2092
South Africa
+2711 628 3200
www.jacana.co.za

© Lindile Xoko, 2021

All rights reserved.

ISBN 978-1-4314-3161-8

Cover design by publicide
Editing by Sean Fraser
Proofreading by Lara Jacob
Set in Sabon 11/16.45pt
Printed by ABC Press
Job no. 003835

See a complete list of Jacana titles at www.jacana.co.za

Contents

Prologue 9
    1. Fuel your idea 13
    2. Start: Fail fast, fail often and fail forward 19
    3. Invest in your ideas 29
    4. Simplify 39
    5. Sell at the speed of currency 59
    6. Run fast 69
    7. Run faster 87
    8. Grow 99
    9. Create an ecosystem of success 115
    10. Solving for X: Defining your formula of success 125
    11. Exit 137
    12. Mindfulness 147
Epilogue 153
'If' 165
Bibliography 167

Prologue

We all have different notions of what success looks like. But the building blocks of success are the same. It is how we assemble those building blocks that determines our outcomes. My years of research and running successful – as well as failed – organisations have informed this playbook. The reality is that we all fail some time. The sooner we realise and accept that failure is a part of the journey to success, the sooner we are able to use it as an instrument to accomplish our goals, the particular, personal "it" that we are working towards.

There are certainties and variables in running a business. The key to getting the outcomes we want lies in converting the variables to certainties. There are basics that can be applied to business to achieve success. In this playbook I outline these basics: from starting a business to optimising it, to growing it and then successfully exiting it. These principles can also be applied to other areas of life where there is a goal to be accomplished.

When I was 15 I started my first profitable business by applying the basics that even a teenager was able to understand and implement. Today, I am writing this as a type of roadmap that my son can one day use to navigate to success – even while experiencing some setbacks. He is only a few months old at this moment, but I would like for him to get the best outcome from every entrepreneurship experience – whether they are victories or losses – because there is success in failure and failure in success. I hope you also find value in this conversation between father and son.

One thing I learned early on in business is that however much you're willing to fail in your pursuit of success is directly proportional to how much you will succeed.

There is a popular saying that "almost 80% of start-ups fail within the first two years". Irrespective of how accurate this is, it's true that most new businesses struggle to become sustainable and often close within a few years. This high failure rate points to three main challenges: a lack of knowledge of how to start a successful business; an inability to grow an organisation; and a failure to become sustainable by navigating changing market conditions.

To enable and empower young entrepreneurs, I have identified a framework for establishing and growing sustainable organisations. I call this *Solving for X: Defining your formula of success*. You can use this framework to set up businesses, grow them, and keep them sustainable – no matter the stage of your business journey.

I have used this model successfully in growing the various businesses I have been fortunate enough to lead. The outcome has always been sustainable growth, but by sharing my business learnings I am hoping to help young entrepreneurs achieve growth and sustainability for their organisations. When those of us who have walked some way as emerging entrepreneurs can share our knowledge in this way, we can look to create a sustainable small business sector and a growing customer base with what Michael E. Porter and Mark R. Kramer call "shared value". They define shared value as "policies and operating practices that enhance the competitiveness of a company while simultaneously advancing economic and social conditions in the communities in which it operates" (Porter and Kramer, 2011).

This goes for all organisations I lead. I use this principle of "shared value" in the very design, where the main goal must achieve a positive societal impact, that is even bigger than what we are doing. Sustainable revenue growth becomes an enabler of that. This means that it has become a capability. This is an ability to start something from absolutely nothing and make it into something great or turning around something that is not quite working well and recreating it into a well-oiled machine. It is a know-how that has been honed over numerous years. This playbook will help you develop that competence so you can achieve your own goals. All that I ask is that you approach this playbook with an open mind, a willingness to put in the work and the discipline to see it all the way through. This is your playbook so feel free to take a pen and scribble all the way through as you make it your own. Enjoy the journey…

1 Fuel your idea

The ideation stage of starting a business is the most exciting, as it presents endless possibilities. This stage is often accompanied by a burst of inspiration, but unfortunately for some people, the journey stops here. This is why it is important to move swiftly from the idea phase into the execution phase. The idea itself is less important because it is all about how well you execute it, and the idea will most likely evolve as you implement it and interact with the market. That is natural. And even a complete pivot is all right – as long as you execute it properly.

Dream as big as your imagination allows, knowing that in order to fulfil those dreams you will have to work harder than the challenges you will face along the way. There is absolutely no limit to what can be achieved. However, it is important to know that big dreams come with big challenges, but potentially big accomplishments, just like small dreams come with small challenges, but also small yields.

What *is* guaranteed is that there will be multiple failures on the path to success. How one views and utilises those failures determines the ultimate outcome. I believe that challenges are stepping stones towards wisdom, happiness and success.

We need to embrace failure from the outset. I would suggest that we should even encourage it, because it creates not only an environment where ideas are valued, but where execution is even more prized. Look to build an environment in which there is no fear of trying new things. This will create a culture of innovation.

Some people do not have the resolve to turn their ideas into reality – hence the old Myles Munroe quote, popularised by Les Brown, that "the graveyard is the richest place on earth, because it is here that you will find all hopes and dreams that were never fulfilled" (Medium, 2021).

There are myriad reasons for this, such as a lack of focus to see the idea through. Or a paralysing fear of failure. Perhaps one lacks the confidence in the idea or confidence in oneself to make the idea a success. Or there may be naysayers, for instance.

At this stage, the idea is a new thought being introduced to old thoughts. And so the battle begins. This is the very first battle the idea must win – win against your old thoughts that have not yet created space for the new thought to be a reality.

Simon Sinek – in his book *Start With Why* – suggests clarifying "why" you want to bring your idea to life. Knowing the reason will fuel your idea. Additionally, because people buy from people, they will more likely relate to the reason behind your idea. This informs your "Vision", which is critical if you want others to buy into your idea. These "others" will include business partners, employees, customers, financiers and so on.

Once the reason why you want to launch your idea is clear to you, you need to find a way of communicating it clearly to the next person. You can sell any idea if you know how to communicate it well. Communication is one of the most useful tools in life. Fortunately, it is also a skill that can be learned and honed – all it takes is practice. So practise daily. For instance, take any opportunity you can get to speak in front of people. Public speaking can be a little intimidating, even terrifying, but the fear gradually dissipates as you become more used to doing it. And doing it repeatedly also improves your craft.

Growing up, I used to be quite shy, but I always tried to speak in public when I got the chance. I would try many different approaches; some would work and some would be absolute failures. But in the process I learned what works for different audiences and how I could use my voice to engage them.

One of the most important lessons I gained from that process was the "Power of Three", which holds that one should communicate no more than three messages in one address, and to find three ways of communicating them. This ensures that you will be understood and remembered by the audience but, most importantly, you'll get the audience to buy into what you're saying. Try to share any more than three messages and you overcrowd your communication. The Power of Three extends to other parts of the *Solving for X: Defining your formula of success* framework. I expand on this in the chapters to come.

Communication is an ongoing requirement, which you will have to keep up: from the idea stage to the operational phase, to the growth phase and so forth. All stakeholders must always be kept sufficiently informed. These will include your customers, your partners, your employees, your suppliers, the community, regulatory bodies, the bank, your board – should you end up having one – and a host of others. Essentially, all parties that impact your organisation or are impacted by it must always be kept informed.

Execution is just as important as communication. This is where your idea starts to become a reality. A focused, energy-driven, rapid-execution model guarantees quick results. Results either validate that you are on the right track, or confirm that further iterations are needed. An execution approach I have used on multiple projects with great success is what I call "Rapid Deployment".

Rapid Deployment turns ideas into reality. It is a model that can move an idea from 0 to 100 in a matter of days. Fast implementation allows the idea to go through an entire life cycle within a short time. Most importantly, it forces you to start.

There are four steps you can take immediately to bring your idea to life. The first is to survey your potential customers, asking whether they would be willing to buy your product or service. Use the survey to determine an appropriate price point, as well as how, when and where they would like to buy the product or service. Further, ask how they would like to be served. Include other questions that will help you understand what will lead to a successful sale. But keep it as simple as possible. Feedback from the survey will give you crucial insights, but also external validation. You can do all of this at absolutely no cost, because you can find free survey tools online.

The second step is to invest real money. This signifies that you are really committed to making the idea a reality. Once you have invested money, you will invest time.

The third step is to identify and engage your dream team. Many hands make light work, but this will also create an environment of collective accountability.

The fourth step is to make incremental progress. I find this is best achieved through daily, 30-minute sprint meetings, daily milestone tracking with the team, and an hour-long checkpoint meeting once a week.

Identifying milestones upfront is important when bringing an idea to life. If you are constantly missing milestones, you need to assess your operating model and the ability of key players to deliver. But you also need to evaluate the milestones themselves to check whether they are realistic or too ambitious. You want to always be slightly ahead of your milestones, as this encourages and fuels your team to achieve even more.

The aim is to get the ball rolling quickly and to start putting points on the scoreboard, because ruminating too long on an idea is the antithesis of progress. It creates room for doubt and discouragement, and it can even mean that you never bring your idea to fruition. You might kick yourself later when someone else launches the idea you've been talking about for years.

2 Start: Fail fast, fail often and fail forward

The best thing to do with an idea is to simply start. Adopt a "fail fast, fail often and fail forward" approach. Ideas by themselves are just thoughts. Execution is what brings them to reality. The sooner you can implement, the sooner you can establish whether your idea is worth rolling out. If it is, then you will start to see positive results early in the process. The reality is that you are not really in business until you have made your first sale. Positive results are great fuel for a team. Before you know it, the team will be self-motivating and driving themselves to achieve even more.

Invest in yourself before you ask anyone else to invest in your idea. At first, this isn't a financial investment. Give your idea 100% of your passion, time and energy. You need to be all-in for your idea to succeed. If you're not completely invested, devoting your time and energy, then you cannot expect anyone else to invest in your idea.

In Rapid Deployment, your goal must be crystal clear. Everyone in the team must have the same understanding of what needs to be achieved and by when. The leader should then define how that goal will be achieved. This must be outlined in simple initiatives that will drive the achievement of the expressed goals.

The initiatives must be built on the Power of Three model. This means asking the question, "What are the three main initiatives that will achieve the best results?" It is easy to list endless activities or initiatives. The trick is to list just five initiatives and weigh them based on impact versus the desired outcome across a specific timeline. Then select the top three with the highest impact or yield.

You will lose focus if there are too many goals, too many initiatives and too much to do. You may even find that you become quite busy, but not much is actually being achieved. Refrain from crowding your priority list, because you might end up chasing your tail.

Once the goal is clear and your priorities for accomplishing that goal are outlined, it's time to start building the right team. Whether you are starting from scratch or already have a team, it is best to focus on team dynamics. Dynamics are critical to how well you work together as a company. It is best to decide what attributes you want in the business and to then structure the team accordingly. The attributes you're looking for must be pointed towards the outcome you would like to realise. Team dynamics also speaks to team health factors such as collective psychology, engagement levels, energy levels and trust. Trust is a significant component of team dynamics – the trust in leadership and the trust from colleagues. Honesty and transparency are values I rate highly in forming strong teams. They create an environment of safety, confidence and dependability. These elements are important to collaboration and also to creating high-performance teams.

The success of a business or a project – especially at an early stage – is down to how great a team you have. Therefore, be deliberate about putting together your dream team. Like an NBA team, a rugby or football team or any sports team, your team will need a variety of specialised skills, but similar well-honed intellects. The market adapts at a rapid rate, so you need strong, sharp minds to make the right decisions quickly.

Your customers must be at the very core of everything you do. Their needs must be your number-one priority. In order to enhance customer experience, try to shorten the customer journey. This calls for strong, fast legs to run fast customer journeys. I don't believe in the model of front office and back office, because that implies that there are employees or team members who are not in sales. In an organisation that's running effectively, everyone is in sales, because all activities are about the customer.

This requires an adaptable, flexible and efficient support structure that acts as the spinal cord of the organisation, a central nervous system that must get immediate feedback from the market and respond accordingly.

There is always a lot of work to do, so you need the right hands for execution. Distribute the workload equitably, in such a way that everyone is contributing real value. But make certain that everyone is focused and working towards the same goal.

If you're not certain how to do this, turn everyone's focus to a particular problem that you are solving. This means that you must sell the problem you solve, and not the product. If you are given the opportunity to solve that problem, your performance should be such that you monopolise the customer's problem – in other words, the customer sees only you (rather than someone else) helping them solve that problem. Everyone in the team should have this mentality.

Every business needs a clear business model before it starts trading. A business model outlines how a business delivers its value. Look to clearly define your business model by answering the following questions:

- What value do we provide?
- Who are we providing it to?
- How and when do we get it to the customer?
- How does a customer get it from us?
- How does the customer know about the value that we provide, as well as how and where to get it?
- What must each person in the organisation do to make sure our value is received by our customers?

The answers to these questions must be clear from inception and need to be reviewed frequently as the business evolves. I expand on these further in Chapter Eight, which is titled "Grow", because these are the same elements you need in order to grow a business. Your business model is the blueprint and map for the success of your business. It must also be adaptable to ever-changing market conditions.

So spend time researching these elements, asking questions, talking to mentors and other organisations that have succeeded in the field you would like to play in. Often, emerging entrepreneurs think their idea is unique and new, but there are few ideas in the world that have not been explored before. Hence the importance of extensive research.

There is, however, nothing wrong with taking an existing idea into the market. In such a case, you simply have to define your unique selling proposition. What will be different about how you deliver value?

If your idea is truly unique and new, then research best practice around how to take a new idea to the market. Study organisations that have achieved what you would like to accomplish, be it an existing or new business model. For example, look at organisations that pioneered a new business model, such as Airbnb, which launched its innovative online home-sharing and vacation-rental marketplace business model in 2008. Then, in 2020, after the Covid-19 pandemic negatively impacted their core business offering, they successfully and quickly pivoted their business model to online experiences. I expand on this in a case study called "Fun, innovation, adapting and high performance" later in this chapter. The case study speaks to the importance of culture in navigating the challenges that organisations face.

Culture must be in the DNA of your organisation. It shapes what you do, how you do it, when you do it – but most importantly why you do it, and how that inspires you to keep doing it better.

Create culture

Culture has always been my special ingredient when establishing high-performance teams. It has allowed the teams that I have led to navigate particularly difficult times and still succeed consistently. Culture is defined by the leader as they set the tone by their actions and their passion for what they do, and why. This defines the vital behaviours of the organisation – not the ones written down somewhere, but the ones that are actually lived. The members of every organisation tend to model their behaviour on the behaviour of their leader.

How a leader communicates the organisation's objectives and the values behind them is central to building a culture that will meet those objectives. As a leader, I've found it speaks volumes to lead by example and to actually walk the talk.

Building a specific team culture must be a deliberate act, because culture forms regardless. If you're not deliberate about building the culture you need, you will end up with a culture that does not embody the behaviours your organisation needs. Here I must warn you that undoing an existing culture is one of the most difficult things you can ever attempt to do in a team. People do not like change, and telling a group of people to change when they have behaved a certain way for a long time goes against human nature. Just think about how difficult it is to change your own set ways and habits. Because it's so hard to change a culture, creating a culture from the outset is the best way to achieve one that meets all your criteria for a successful team. It's important to also create a self-sustaining, self-healing culture that will evolve. A culture rooted in accountability and responsibility, but one that is driven by a higher purpose.

These are the elements you need to create a self-sustaining and self-healing culture:

One: Define a unifying purpose. Essentially, this is "why we do what we do"; the reason everyone wakes up in the morning and gives their best every minute of the day. This is something your people think about and live, even outside work hours, because it is bigger than just the nine-to-five. It is part of the reason they're on this planet. It is aligned to their purpose – or better yet, it *is* their purpose.

Two: Bring together great team members who know how they contribute to the purpose. They must understand how their purpose converges with that of the team or the organisation. This creates a sense of belonging, of community and a feeling of working for something bigger than oneself.

Three: Shared values and common ground must be outlined, as this is the cornerstone of culture, one that is self-sustaining and self-healing. A common purpose unifies, because it creates an environment where values can be lived as well as draw from personal values. If there is common ground, there will be common understanding.

Four: Once the values are established, the vital behaviours that uphold those values must be defined. These are the common behaviours that the team must live every single day in order to work towards the common purpose.

Five: Once the vital behaviours are defined, the core behaviours must be turned into rituals. Repetition is the mother of learning, so rituals are those repetitive activities that reaffirm the vital behaviours and validate the values. The rituals must be done in such a way that they are rewarding in themselves.

Six: It is imperative that rewards and penalties for particular behaviours are defined and aligned to the purpose. It is human nature to repeat something for which you are rewarded and to curb behaviour for which you are penalised. This is simply conditioning, which we experience from the moment we are born. Team conditioning is part of building successful teams.

Seven: To drive accountability and ownership, every team member must feel empowered. It's the leader's job to ensure that the goal is clearly understood by everyone. Trust is thus a key component. As leader, you need to trust that each person has the best interests of the business, division or project at heart, and feels empowered to make decisions in their area of expertise and then execute them. This also requires that roles, responsibilities and parameters be clearly outlined.

Eight: Diverse thoughts or divergent ideas should be welcome at all times. This keeps the culture open-minded, with constant fresh thinking. Taking team members' ideas into consideration and valuing them fosters continuous improvement. It also creates an atmosphere of psychological safety for team members. Harvard Business School professor, Amy Edmondson, defines psychological safety as "a belief that one will not be punished or humiliated for speaking up with ideas, questions, concerns or mistakes" (Impraise, 2021).

Nine: To bring it all together, there must be a clear daily visualisation of what success looks like. When we are winning, what do we look like, talk like, walk like? When we experience difficulty, how do we pull together to overcome it?

Below is an example of the importance of culture. This is a case study about Airbnb, which experienced severe challenges and revenue loss due to the Covid-19 pandemic. However, they instituted a quick turnaround, which included a business-model pivot, ultimately pulling off the best initial public offering (IPO) in the pandemic year of 2020. The case underlines the importance of culture in navigating challenges and continuing to win.

Case study: Fun, innovation, adapting and high performance

Airbnb is a great example of an organisation with a culture of innovation and high performance. Airbnb was valued at a healthy $31 billion prior to the Covid-19 pandemic, but that valuation dropped by 16% to $26 billion after the pandemic broke.

Research and analysis firm AirDNA found that Airbnb's valuation had dropped even further to $18 billion by April 2020 – almost half its initial value. Bookings in Beijing dropped by 96% from January to March as the virus spread through China. In the same period, Europe's short-term rental business fell by up to 80%, and in major US cities such as New York, San Francisco and Seattle revenue was down by more than 50%. The organisation had to lay off about 25% of its employees, and forecasts projected things would get even bleaker.

Fast forward to 06h52, 11 December 2020. Tyler Sonnemaker writes in a *Business Insider* article that "Airbnb is worth more than 3 hotel giants combined after its stock popped 143% on first trading day"! Airbnb's valuation had surged to around $86.5 billion, after closing at $144.71 per share – more than twice its initial offering of $68 per share (Business Insider, 2020).

This shows some of the benefits of being a data-driven organisation. A data-driven organisation is effective at collecting data across all facets of the business, allowing for complete and effective decision-making. This kind of an organisation does not operate on assumptions, gut feel or incomplete data to make decisions. Because Airbnb is a data-driven organisation, it was able to adapt its strategy. In April, the organisation introduced new features aimed at longer-term stays. The data showed that this was a growing part of its business, and the Airbnb decision-makers were determined to capitalise on that. The pandemic had had a negative effect on travel, which meant that short-term rentals had suffered greatly. The company also quicky switched its offering to include "Experiences" – offerings that include hiking tours and cooking classes.

Thanks to interventions such as these, as well as cost-cutting tactics, Airbnb was able to announce a surprise $219.3 million profit in the third quarter of 2020.

Airbnb was founded by Brian Chesky, Joe Gebbia and Nathan Blecharczyk in 2007 – even renting air mattresses in their apartment as a way to make rent. They have built a culture of "belonging everywhere", which extends to employees, hosts and guests. The culture of belonging creates a community of open dialogue, empathy and understanding. This means that the success of the organisation belongs to everyone. For this reason, when Airbnb decided to pivot, not only did everyone in the community come along, they played a part in pivoting the company to the new innovation, flexibility and high performance. And they had fun while doing it.

Airbnb's Global Head of Employee Experience, Mark Levy, says: "At the end of the day, we want everyone in our company to have experienced the journey and understanding of what it's like to belong anywhere, through the eyes of the host and the guest" (Culture Amp, 2020).

To succeed, you must first start. For a business, the value of starting is that the market waits for no one. So start and aim to sell just one of whatever it is that you sell. Just one unit, because once you have sold to one customer, there is no reason you should not sell to a thousand. And once you have sold to a thousand, then you can sell to ten thousand!

So start! Then immediately begin with what I term "Rapid Replication and Proliferation", because time is never on your side. Rapid replication and proliferation is to quickly find out what works, and then rapidly replicate and scale it to penetrate the market. This also involves quickly identifying what *doesn't* work, then rapidly discarding it so you can focus on what does work.

3 Invest in your ideas

What determines a company's success is a business model that has been well defined and then executed. But what decides the yield is the input. By that, I mean the investment of time, money and resources. The sooner you understand that no one owes you anything, the better. Again, remember that you need to invest in yourself before you can ask anyone else to do so. There is no reward without risk. That means you must put in the time, the money and the resources – to the limits of your capabilities – to achieve the best yield that those can afford. Only when you have proven that the business model works and that it has demonstrable yield, can you start to approach others to invest their time, money and resources into your venture.

There is a variety of ways that you can do this once you reach this stage of success. As the old proverb goes, "Success begets success." This also requires that you own this part of your success and the yield that comes with it. This positions you well for the next phase of your growth when you take on board additional funders. You will not be so desperate that you end up accepting bad commercial arrangements. When you accept desperate terms, debt is often so high and interest rates so unreasonable that you end up working for the funder and not for your customer, your business or yourself. This is not sustainable or healthy – for your business or for yourself.

Bootstrapping

The best way to raise funds for your business is to actually sell the problem that it solves. You can sell your product even before it has been completed by sourcing a number of friendly customers and getting them to buy the product for delivery at an agreed future date. Or you could sell a minimum viable product, meaning that, although it has not been finalised, it has the basic functionality. You can evolve the product with the support of the first adopters of your product, using their payments to fund that stage of your product development.

This is called bootstrapping, and there are numerous companies that have used this approach. GoPro used this model and achieved a $3 billion valuation at its initial public offering (IPO). GitHub, the software-development platform, was also launched as a bootstrapped start-up in 2008. Ten years later, it sold to Microsoft for $7.5 billion.

Bootstrapping means building a business with little to no outside finance – using only the money coming in from the first sales, as well as personal savings. This requires the business to run in a lean manner, keeping overheads as low as possible and maximising profits from personal investments.

You can explore various bootstrapping methodologies to limit outside debt and equity financing. This might mean using your own savings and income to finance business operations. You could, for instance, use your personal credit card. Effort – sometimes called sweat equity – is another way to invest in your start-up. As mentioned earlier, time is valuable. It's also imperative that you keep your operating costs as low as possible, so as not to put too much pressure on cashflow. Start-ups and smaller organisations need available cash, so avoid keeping any more inventory than you need to fulfil your orders. If you need to keep inventory, minimise it by moving it quickly so your stockholding doesn't hold your cashflow to ransom. You should also explore the myriad government subsidies and grants that are available to small businesses. Ultimately, look to sell at the speed of currency. This will be explained in greater detail in Chapter Five.

Vendor financing

If you are dependent on the sales of your product to pay your suppliers, then how you negotiate payment terms with your suppliers will make all the difference. For example, we know that sometimes payments to small companies are slow in coming. So, if your suppliers are pushing for payments but you have not been paid by your own customers, this puts immense pressure on your cashflow. You also don't want to mess with your business's ability to get credit: defaulting on payments is not an option, because this reduces your credit score.

Understand how sales cycles and payment cycles work in your organisation and base your forecasts on these. Plan inventory and sales accordingly. Once you have a clear projection, sit with your vendors to negotiate the appropriate payment terms. Treat your suppliers like partners. Most vendors will have standard 30-day payment terms. As a small business, look to negotiate longer payment terms, so that you can ease pressure on your cashflow. This is an effective way to finance your company, because it means you can start sales even before you have paid for supplies. The vendor is financing *you!*

Self-funding channels

Find more established channel partners that are good at sales, who are experienced and willing to sell your product at risk. "At risk" means your channel partner sells your product or service at no cost to you and they are then paid upon a completed sale. This is also called the full-risk or own-risk model. In Chapter Eight, we go into the detail of how you can use the model to grow your business.

This model is, however, contingent on how exciting and well priced your product or service is, as well as how quickly your partner can fulfil orders. Your partner is fully dependent on how well the product sells, driven by demand and speed of sales. Therefore, if this model is to succeed, your customer-experience processes need to be great.

You can also adopt a shared-risk or partial-risk model, where you split the risk with your channel partners. Here, you pay a fraction of what you would ordinarily pay, and the rest is paid upon conclusion of sale. You can also extend this to your sales staff, where you pay a lower basic salary, but offer massive rewards upon conclusion of sales. However, for this to work, confidence in your product needs to be high, because you are also rewarding and incentivising your staff to convert sales. The rewards model needs to be generous in order to attract the best talent.

You can also employ referral partners, who earn a percentage for referring successful sales leads to your business.

Project or campaign loans

Find a bank or financing partner that is willing to finance your project or campaign. Usually, funders are willing to provide finance as long as you have a purchase order and a payment schedule. But you need to negotiate the terms upfront. This means proactively mapping your business model and then sitting with the funder to explain it to them. Share your sales forecast and negotiation terms should you win the business or the contract. This is so that you merely activate it at the time that you need to.

If you are reactive rather than proactive, you will be pressed for time and, with a desperate need to access cash, you may just accept any deal – even if it is unreasonable or not in your own best interests. Your desperation may force you to accept high interest rates or outrageous payment terms that will put further pressure on you and eat into your profits. I have seen this happening quite often, where because of the need to preserve some shred of credibility, a small business accepts a less-than-ideal finance deal where they do not even make a profit.

Some businesses are prepared to make a loss so that they save face, because they know that if they do not deliver, they might never get another opportunity with that client. Short-term microlenders know this and take advantage of these reactive entrepreneurs, sometimes charging up to 50% interest or more. I have even stepped in to help some small businesses that were under time pressure to deliver. I helped out, not by loaning them money – because I do not operate as a bank – but by delivering on their behalf and paying them a referral fee. In all these cases, the small business made more money than they would have if they had accepted an expensive loan and tried to deliver on their own.

Believe it or not, raising funding is closely aligned to your personality, your inclination and your skills. It is easier for me to raise funding through selling, because I am good at sales. I can also raise funding via the value chain by being creative in how I negotiate with suppliers and partners around service or product delivery. My skills in this area probably come from my not having a lot of money growing up, having to maximise what I had, and to use it without spending it. In cases like mine, a former disadvantage can become an advantage. Don't let that go to waste. Try to be creative and have fun with it. The process of raising funds to grow your firm can be quite exciting.

Crowdfunding

Some people are better at crowdfunding, for example. On crowdfunding, trader Tim Smith said in an article titled "Crowdfunding", dated 7 September 2020, that:

> Crowdfunding is the use of small amounts of capital from a large number of individuals to finance a new business venture. Crowdfunding makes use of the easy accessibility of vast networks of people through social media and crowdfunding websites to bring investors and entrepreneurs together, with the potential to increase entrepreneurship by expanding the pool of investors beyond the traditional circle of owners, relatives and venture capitalists (Smith, 2021).

Crowdfunding has expanded funding options for entrepreneurs, because now anyone with an idea, a project or a campaign can pitch to many people at once and offer them investment opportunities that are well within their means. There has been an increase in crowdfunding websites and digital platforms, the most popular being Kickstarter and Indiegogo.

Indiegogo has started offering fundraising campaigns without end dates. Afrikstart, another platform, aims to connect African entrepreneurs with funders worldwide. I would recommend researching platforms before you decide which will be right for your needs and goals.

Some people are better at raising debt through banks. I see how necessary this is, but it is not my personal preference. Banks are primarily in it for themselves and how much they can make in return. This is a basic business imperative for them, so you can expect sky-high fees and interest rates, as well as unforgiving time pressures to return their money with the agreed fees. This is fair, in that the degree of abuse is agreed upon upfront, and, as long as all parties play their parts, then it's amicable. But if things don't go according to plan – as is quite often the case in entrepreneurship – it can be quite painful. Taking on debt from banks is a route I would only recommend for more established organisations, because negotiations are then likely to be on a more even keel. Unfortunately, a big-versus-small dynamic skews the balance of power towards the bigger entity – the bank, in this case. More often than not, the small business is heavily disadvantaged.

Having gone this route myself, my suggestion is that if it's the only available option, the best way is to be prepared to absorb the debt into the business. For example, you have to make sure that your gearing is correct. Gearing is a measure of your company's financial leverage – the degree to which your organisation's activities are funded by shareholders' funds versus creditors' funds. Therefore, gearing refers to your debt-to-equity ratio.

You *must* minimise the risk of losing your assets. Remember that a bank loan is usually sanctioned against collateral, which may include business or personal assets. Trust me, banks can get quite thuggish when it's time to collect. Don't let the suits fool you.

Equity

Speaking of equity, another option for raising capital is through the sale of shares in your company. Equity financing comes with an ownership interest for the shareholders. This may involve selling a few shares in your organisation in order to raise a few thousand rand from a private investor. Or it might be a stock-exchange listing or IPO worth billions. In Chapter 11 we will expand on IPOs.

I prefer partnering with development finance institutions (DFIs). The OECD describes DFIs as:

> ... specialised development banks or subsidiaries set up to support private sector development in developing countries. They are usually majority-owned by national governments

and source their capital from national or international development funds or benefit from government guarantees. This ensures their creditworthiness, which enables them to raise large amounts of money on international capital markets and provide financing on very competitive terms (OECD, 2021).

There are various benefits to partnering with DFIs, including favourable commercial terms, because they have a mainly developmental mandate. They also often offer end-to-end support, to make sure that you succeed and they improve their impairment rates.

Alternative methods of raising funding

Angel investors
With the right kind of networking, you may be able to access angel investors. These are people on the lookout for the next business in which to invest. Angel investor deals almost always involve you accepting funds in exchange for equity. In the early stages of business, we are often very attached to our companies and are reluctant to even consider giving away equity. We may think of equity in terms of future value and be wary of giving away too much.

One of my business regrets is that I turned away angel investors for fear of letting go of equity. Later, we ended up going the bank route to finance our expansion, which was not without trouble. Angel investment can definitely work, as long as you protect yourself by means of clear contractual agreements on how to exit your investors. It is also good to partner with the right angel investor, one that will enable the business objectives while still giving you enough space to do what you need to do. Angel investors can also offer mentorships and access to a wider network and potential customers.

Venture capitalists
Another alternative is venture capitalists. These are individuals or firms with money to invest in start-ups with high growth potential. They also look for a share of equity in exchange for their investment, but are also usually looking to be involved in the direction of your company.

There is a plethora of funding paths and models. I recommend that you research the various models and decide which funding route best suits your personality, your inclination and your skills.

I have often said that the instruments in most funding institutions are archaic and need to be modernised to accommodate the evolving needs of small enterprises. Business models have transformed to meet the changing needs of customers and the market, but funding models have remained the same. This not only hurts the small-business sector, but the financing institutions themselves – they often have impairment rates north of 70%. That cannot be sustainable for the small-to-medium enterprise (SME) sector, and I daresay it shows we are going backwards in the structured-funding space.

I encourage you to investigate the impairment rates of the institutions from which you are requesting funding. Because their funding models are generally faulty, they often end up funding the wrong organisations with the wrong funding instruments. Their recovery rates then suffer, and they become risk averse, curtailing funding to the very firms they should be funding – innovative organisations with massive growth potential that would provide better recovery rates and reduced impairment.

Such conservative lending behaviour makes the entire sector suffer. Unfortunately, unethical entrepreneurs will often take advantage of these lenders – with little intention of paying back loans. The ability of funding institutions to recover is not great, and debt often ends up being written off.

But don't take my word for it. Perhaps I don't have the

personality, inclination or skills to raise funds through this method. I say that with a chuckle, but what I do know is that simplicity underpins success.

4 Simplify

Simplicity is at the very heart of success because, *when you simplify how you understand your business, you simplify how your customers see the value you offer them.* At its core, the model for this formula asks three simple but fundamental questions, as illustrated in Figure 1. By asking *why* you do what you do, *what* you actually do and *how* you do what you do, the model encourages you to outline reasons compelling enough to start and grow a sustainable firm and navigate the challenges of entrepreneurship.

Why you do what you do determines why you should succeed.

Secondly, the questions force you to delineate a clear, succinct answer of what the business actually does. We often take this for granted and so we miss it completely. Thirdly, an enterprise involves doing things for particular people at specific times and places for the appropriate price. Therefore, *how* you do what you do is pivotal, if these people are to keep asking you to do what you do for them. Additionally, you need to do things so well that even more people ask you to do it for them.

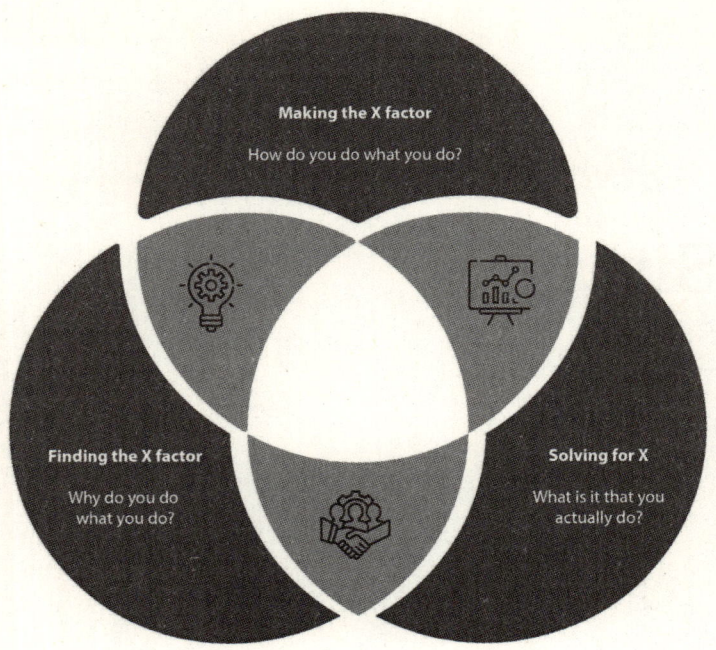

Figure 1: *Solving for X model*

The first two questions determine how the business should be organised and service its customers. The model then poses a set of prompting questions and derives a formula for success as shown in Figure 2.

Why do you do what you do?

Asking why you do what you do forces you to put the person you're doing it for at the centre of that question. If you are a business, then that is the customer. Without a customer, the business does not exist. It is merely a concept. To give your business meaning, you have to put the customer at the centre of everything you do. You do that by having a detailed understanding of your customer. This insight will equip you to add inimitable value to your customer. But first you have to know who your customer is.

WHY (Y)	WHAT (Z)	HOW (X)
Who is the customer?	Objective	What are our core competencies?
What do they need?		What are our competitive advantages?
Why do they need/want it?		What other competencies should we build?
What are they willing to pay?		
How do they want it?		What other competitive advantages should we establish?
When do they want it?		Do our core/established competencies and competitive advantages stand the test of time?
What customers do you have?		
What customers do you want to keep?		$X = Y + Z$
Which customers do you want?		$X^2 + Z^2 = Y^2$
What does the customer you want look like in 2, 5, 10 years time?		$\therefore Y^2 = \text{Revenue}^2$

Figure 2: The model

Who is the customer?
At the time of writing in 2020, the world population stood at 7.8 billion (2020) – 7 832 504 383, to be exact, according to worldometers.info. It would be rare that your product or service is for all of those people. So, knowing the value you provide requires that you define exactly who the value is for.

What do they need?
So that you do not miss the target customer, it is imperative to know exactly what the customers' needs are. This requires that you actually walk the journey of the customer, to gain a nuanced understanding of your customer's expressed and unexpressed needs or wants.

Why do they need/want it?
Much like your own *why* must be clear, so must the *why* of your customer. Where these two collide is where the sale happens. When *why* they want it coincides with *why* you do it, this creates a value

bubble where passion, multiplied by capability, meets the need, and quality is achieved.

What are they willing to pay for it?
Making sure that the value is clear – and the customer who needs that value is defined – must be followed by knowing how much the customer is willing to pay for it. The best way of finding this out is to actually ask the customer. That could be done through focus groups – groups of people assembled to contribute in a discussion about a product or service before it is launched.

How do they want it?
It is not enough to merely have a product and a price, or even knowledge of who your customer is. You also need to know where your customer is; how and where they'd like to pay for your product or service; and where they would like to receive it. This speaks to the distribution channels you need to use to serve your customers as they prefer – in other words, digital, call centre, store, home or office. There are many other distribution points or sales channels you can deploy to serve your customers. This underpins your go-to-market strategy.

Airfocus defines a go-to-market strategy as:

> … a plan of how a company is going to release a product after it has been developed and how it will be sold and promoted within the marketplace. The strategy is one that uses the internal and external resources of a business, advertises the overarching value of the product, and attempts to gain a competitive advantage in the market over its competitors (Airfocus, 2020).

The topic of sales channels and distribution models is fleshed out further in Chapter Eight.

When do they want it?
In the age of instant gratification, it is important to know when your customer would like to receive the value that you provide. Sometimes it may not matter if you have the product or even service at the right price because if you cannot provide it when the customer needs it or wants it, they may move on to a competitor who *can* provide it when they need it.

What customers do you have?
Customer experience speaks to the ease with which your customer can buy from you. Capability speaks to how easily you can provide that product and service. Where those two intersect, growth is achieved. This also speaks to scale, and as a start-up or small business, this must always be calibrated correctly.

I explained this concept in June 2018 on *The Big Small Business Show* hosted by Allon Raiz on Business Day TV. Andile Khumalo, then chief investment officer of MSG Afrika, and I were discussing the MTN Business and MSG Afrika "I am an Entrepreneur" workshops that year. The video can be found on the Business Day TV YouTube channel.

At that time, I was acting general manager for small and medium businesses at MTN Business, and I spoke about the importance of timing for small companies. This refers to capability versus yield, where too much capacity and low yield can make the cost of service too high and thus break the bank. The inverse is where the yield or demand for your product or service is too high, but the capacity to deliver is low. This means your product/service quality is compromised, and you end up breaking yourself trying to provide value despite the difficulties – just so you can get paid. This is also not sustainable.

If you already have a customer base, ask yourself which type of customers are costing you too much to service, and which ones cost you less and are less difficult to serve. These questions may also be applied to the number of customers. For example, how many customers are too many for you to serve with the capacity you have? Or, what is the appropriate number for you to serve with your current capacity?

This will buy you time to organically build the capacity to coincide with the growth in customers or even customer types. The best way to test capacity versus yield is to calculate the indicator Cost of Sales, or Cost of Goods Sold, which Investopedia defines as:

> the direct costs of producing the goods sold by a company. This amount includes the cost of the materials and labour directly used to create the good. It excludes indirect expenses, such as distribution costs and sales force costs (Fernando, 2021).

If you already have a base, it is important to ask the following questions to know your customer:

Which customers do you want to keep?
This is not an easy question to answer honestly, because it is easy to be fooled by revenue if that customer is paying you. But the true measure is profitability. How easy or difficult is it for you to serve that customer, and how much is it costing you? You can test this by doing what I call the "Follow the money" exercise. If you deliver a physical product, we can use a can of soft drink to illustrate the point.

You need to follow that can from source to destination. Take into account how much you pay for it. Let's say you buy it for R8.75. You then also need to calculate how much you pay for transporting it from your suppliers to your store.

Let's say a case of 24 cans is R209.95, and you have bought 10 cases, which cost you R2 099.50. You pay R500 for delivery. Then you pay R2.08 for each can. When you add that R2.08 to R8.75, you get R10.83. Then you must also factor in the storage cost for the time it is waiting to be bought.

If you pay R5000 storage per month, you're paying R166.67 per day in a 30-day month. That's R0.69 storage/rent per can per day. If that soft drink can sits on the shelf for 10 days, it incurs R6.90 in storage costs. R6.90 plus R10.83 equals R17.73 in costs. If your salesperson earns R2 500 a month, then it costs you R3.47 to have them sell that can, and R3.47 plus R17.73 means that the cost to sell that can is R21.20.

Let's say you retail the can for R9.99. Your loss on that soft drink is R11.21!

This means your cost of sale and distribution is too high. But if you only look at how much you pay to buy it (R8.75) and how much you sell it for (R9.99), you may get the (incorrect) impression that you have a profitable product and customer.

Which customers do you want?
It has been said time and again that you cannot be all things to all people. This applies perfectly in business where you do not have the capacity to fulfil everyone's needs and wants all the time. It is best to be selective and play to your strengths.

Being clear about which customers you serve with your value proposition and how many customers you can support with your capability has more benefits.

The first benefit is that you will be able to create focus. It should then be easier to answer the questions of what, why, who, when and how. You can also sharpen the skills you need in order to deliver the solution better than your competitors. Aim to be the best in one area, rather than average in a couple of areas. As mentioned, the latter is costly, with minimum yield, whereas the former has better returns.

Moreover, focus allows you to have a clear message and positioning for your product or service. With targeted marketing, the communication and sales channels become clearer, which in turn leads to more accurate messaging and sales initiatives that generate more sales.

It is certainly all right for your target market to evolve or even expand as your strengths grow. Once you establish competencies, strengths and competitive advantages, you can leverage these to build others and even diversify value proposition.

However, the strategy is to stay loyal to your focus, because that strengthens your value chain. Technical editor Carla Tardi outlines the elements of a value chain thus:

> Firstly, a value chain is a step-by-step business model for transforming a product or service from idea to reality. Secondly, value chains help increase a business's efficiency so the business can deliver the most value for the least possible cost. Thirdly, the end goal of a value chain is to create a competitive advantage for a company by increasing productivity while keeping costs reasonable (Tardi, 2020).

Competitive advantages are essential to your success and later we will go into much more detail about how to create and sustain competitive advantages.

But first, what *is* a competitive advantage? Business writer Alexandra Twin describes competitive advantage as elements that enable an organisation to "produce goods or services better or more cheaply than its rivals". These elements position the organisation "to generate more sales or superior margins compared to its market rivals" (Twin, 2020).

What does the customer you want look like in two, five, ten years' time?
Ideally, you will get to know your customer so well that you can project how they evolve – and how their needs evolve – over time. Change is a natural part of life, and the sooner you embrace it, the better you'll be able to navigate it and innovate around it. Ask your customer what they expect their life to be like in one year, two, three and so forth. Overlay that with your own analysis of

your firm, which will of course include a detailed understanding of your customer.

Use these insights to define how your value proposition will evolve in line with the changing needs and wants of your customer/s. This will ensure that you are not left behind by your customers and the market. Keep looking to innovate, to find better, more cost-effective ways to delight your customers. Find new ways to constantly deliver the best value efficiently to your customers. This will mean constantly reviewing your business model, the processes, your go-to-market strategy and the technologies you need to deliver your offers in the best possible way.

You will also need to look at the employees that help you deliver. Ask yourself whether you have the right team or specific team members to continue to deliver at the highest level. This will affect the training you give your team, because it has to suit the outcome you desire for the customers.

How do you do what you do?

How you do what you do is directly informed by what you must do, why, for whom and when. Most importantly, it talks to what you are actually capable of doing. In business, capability is a basic element of success. If mastered, it leads to competitive advantage. As Jack Welch said in his book *Winning*, "If you don't have a competitive advantage, don't compete" (Welch and Welch, 2006).

So, let us discuss how to create that competitive advantage.

In *The Discipline of Market Leaders*, Michael Treacy and Fred Wiersema outline three areas where your advantage could be established. The first is customer experience; the second is operational excellence; and the third is a leading value proposition. It is best to look at these from a customer's point of view.

History tells us that the best products or services are those that customers did not even know they needed, but once they get them, they suddenly can't believe they could ever live without them.

These new offerings are so valuable that they indelibly improve the customer's life, and paying for them becomes an easy decision. Hence the name "value proposition".

Take stock of the competencies you have, with the aim of converting them into competitive advantages and a value proposition. To do this, we must go back to the basic principles of establishing a business model and base the requisite competencies on them.

Table 1: Fundamentals of your business model translated into competencies

Basic principle	Competency
What value do we provide?	Your *product or service*
Who are we providing it to?	Your *customer*
How and when do we get it to the customer?	Your *distribution models*
How does a customer get it from us?	Your *channel model*
How does the customer know about the value that we provide, and how and where to get it?	Your *marketing* model
What must each person in the organisation do to make sure our value is received by our customers?	Your *operating model and culture*

Once you have established your competencies, you will need a model to test whether they give your organisation a sustained competitive advantage. Here, we can use the VRIO framework – a strategy tool devised by Jay Barney in 1991 to help organisations identify competencies that give them sustained competitive advantages. We will come back to the competencies outlined in Table 1, as we apply the VRIO framework.

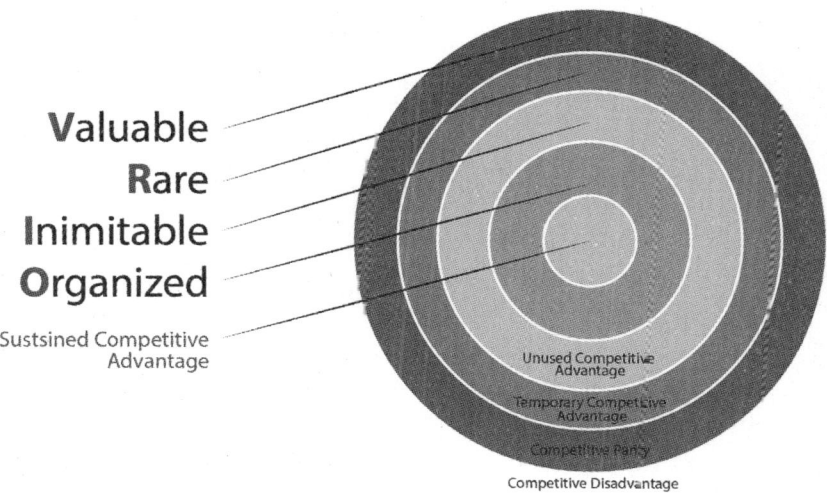

Figure 3: VRIO model (ClearPointstrategy.com, 2020)

Rachel Smith, of ClearPoint Strategy, advises that the framework should be applied *after* **you've created a vision statement,** but *before* the strategic planning process. This is because the advantages you identify will inform how you approach the market and the direction your organisation should take.

> VRIO is an acronym for a four-question framework of value, rarity, imitability and organisation. The four components of VRIO analysis are typically approached in the style of a decision tree:
>
> **Value:** Do you offer a resource that adds value for customers? Are you able to exploit an opportunity or neutralise competition with an internal capability?
> **No:** You are at a *competitive disadvantage* and need to reassess your resources and capabilities to uncover value.
> **Yes:** If value is established, move on in your VRIO analysis to rarity.

Rarity: Do you control scarce resources or capabilities? Do you own something that's hard to find, yet in demand?

No: You have value, but lack rarity, putting your company in a position of *competitive parity*. Your resources are valuable but common, which makes competing in the marketplace more challenging (but not impossible). It's recommended to go back one step and reassess.

Yes: With value and rarity identified, your next hurdle is imitability.

Imitability: Is it expensive to duplicate your organisation's resources or capability? Is it difficult to find an equivalent substitute to compete with your offerings?

No: If your resource has value and rarity, but is affordable or easy to copy, you have a *temporary competitive advantage*. It will require considerable effort to stay ahead of competitors and differentiate your services – go back one step and reassess.

Yes: You offer something that's valuable, rare and hard to imitate – now the focus is on your organisation.

Organisation: Does your company have organised management systems, processes, structures and the culture to capitalise on resources and capabilities?

No: Without the internal organisation and support, it will be difficult to fully realise the potential of your valuable, rare and costly-to-imitate resources. Your company will have an *unused competitive advantage* and will need to reassess how to attain the needed organisation.

Yes: Your company has achieved the ultimate goal of *sustained competitive advantage* when it has successfully identified all four components of the VRIO framework (ClearPointstrategy.com, 2020).

If you are successful in identifying all four components of the VRIO framework, then you have achieved a sustained competitive advantage. Now, let's refer back to the competencies outlined in Table 1 and apply them to the VRIO model. Of course, you can identify other competencies in your own organisation that are relevant in your specific industry. These are merely the basic competencies that you need in order to design a business model.

What are your core competencies?
Charles Crawford defines a competency as:

> a set of particular abilities and knowledge that sets a company apart from its competitors. Certain combinations of qualities and characteristics, often called core competencies, can allow a company to thrive in its market segment and greatly outpace its competitors in terms of earnings and customer satisfaction. In highly successful companies, core competencies have most likely developed in areas where they add the most value to products (Crawford, 2020).

Thus, to create competitive advantages, you need to establish competencies. Figure 4 provides a framework you can use to outline your competencies.

	Your company					Your main competitor					Your secondary competitor				
Competencies	Value	Rarity	Inimitability	Organisation	Advantage	Value	Rarity	Inimitability	Organisation	Advantage	Value	Rarity	Inimitability	Organisation	Advantage
product or service															
Customer															
Distribution models															
Channel model															
Marketing model															
Culture															
Other competency															
Other competency															
Other competency															
Other competency															
Other competency															
Other competency															
Other competency															

Figure 4: *Applying the VRIO model to your organisation*

Figure 5 is an example of Amazon's VRIO analysis. You can use this example to identify competencies in your own organisation or industry.

What are your competitive advantages?
To acquire and retain more customers, yield more revenue and profits or achieve more brand loyalty, you need to establish a sustainable competitive advantage – or a few. Therefore, endeavour to build an edge in very specific but highly impactful areas, namely: value proposition, customer experience, distribution model, marketing and culture. These areas answer the five basic questions of setting up a successful operating model. What value you provide; to whom; how you get it to the customer; and how you tell them about the value and where they can get it.

It's also about how well you provide that value to your customers.

Amazon's Organisational Resources and Capabilities	V	R	I	O
Growing brick-and-mortar presence	✓			
Growing diversity of online services	✓			
Growing portfolio of private label products	✓			
Extensive delivery network involving domestic, regional and international partnerships	✓	✓		
Expertise based on a considerable history of e-commerce	✓	✓		
Strategic warehouses and distributions hubs	✓	✓		
Sustained Competitive Advantage(s):				
High global brand equity	✓	✓	✓	✓
High market capitalisation	✓	✓	✓	✓
International network of affiliates that expand international market reach	✓	✓	✓	✓
Artificial intelligence capabilities	✓	✓	✓	✓

Figure 5: *Amazon's VRIO Analysis (White, 2019)*

Having created competencies in these areas, you need to ensure that they are valuable, rare and difficult to imitate, and that your firm is organised to benefit from the valuable, rare and inimitable competencies.

What other competencies should you build?

It is essential to always take stock of your organisational competencies – especially if your business is considering pivoting, diversifying or instituting some other change. Being mindful of your firm's strategic direction means understanding which competencies you have, and which will ensure success.

The strategic direction may include diversification of your products and services, a new costing model, or augmenting your entire business model. Once you have audited your organisational competencies and know which you need, you need to start establishing those strengths. You create these core competencies by investing in the capabilities most valued by the customer and aiming to do them better than any other player.

Try to stay small and agile. Scale though innovation, but hit harder and faster and more accurately all the time. The age of the mega-corporation has shown that it's getting harder to innovate as a big organisation. Whenever you find yourself getting bigger and slower, you will need to revise, redefine and refresh your competencies and competitive advantages.

What other competitive advantages should you establish?
As the business grows or changes, it must continually assess its competitive advantages, as well as its core competencies. This is to sharpen the edge that draws customers to you rather than your competitors.

It is also important to note that, in a way, you compete against yourself. Your success competes against your ultimate failure. So your competitive advantage is the difference between a customer choosing you or not. This is why you must continually redefine your competitive advantages.

Do your core, established competencies and competitive advantages stand the test of time?
You need to future-proof your competitive advantages. External factors – market conditions, competitive landscape, gross domestic product, inflation, unemployment, for instance – evolve over time, and you need to ensure that your internal strengths continue to prevail as external conditions change.

This *sustainable competitive advantage* involves scalability, adaptability and elasticity. Scalability is the ability of a firm to adjust to increased scope or workload. Adaptability is the ability to adjust to new conditions. Adam Hayes defines elasticity as:

> a measure of a variable's sensitivity to a change in another variable, most commonly this sensitivity is the change in price relative to changes in other factors. In business and economics, elasticity refers to the degree to which

individuals, consumers or producers change their demand or the amount supplied in response to price or income changes. It is predominantly used to assess the change in consumer demand as a result of a change in a good or service's price (Hayes, 2020).

To navigate your ever-changing business context, stay acutely aware of the competencies that create sustainable competitive advantages and constantly refine them.

What is it that you actually do?

So, what is it that you actually do?

Charles Revson, founder of Revlon, one of the biggest beauty brands in the world, summed up what they actually do when he said: "In the factory, we make cosmetics, in the store we sell hope" (Tobias, 1983).

That is putting the customer at the centre of what you do, why you do it and how you do it! When asked what you actually do, it is easy to fall into the cliché of talking about the product, service or their features. What you do is actually determined by *who* you do it for and *why*.

Another great example of a company that puts the customer first is Amazon. Its mission is to be the most customer-centric company on earth. They expand on this mission when they say:

> Our mission is to continually raise the bar of the customer experience by using the internet and technology to help consumers find, discover and buy anything, and empower businesses and content creators to maximise their success (Amazon, 2020).

As mentioned before, Airbnb also lives its mission when it states:

Airbnb's mission is to create a world where anyone can belong anywhere, and we are focused on creating an end-to-end travel platform that will handle every part of your trip (Airbnb, 2019).

An example I use, and one that inspires me very much comes from the 'Think Different' Apple commercial narrated by Steve Jobs:

Here's to the crazy ones, the misfits, the rebels, the troublemakers, the round pegs in the square holes … the ones who see things differently – they're not fond of rules … You can quote them, disagree with them, glorify or vilify them, but the only thing you can't do is ignore them, because they change things … They push the human race forward, and while some may see them as the crazy ones, we see genius, because the ones who are crazy enough to think that they can change the world, are the ones who do (Jobs, 1997).

The approach here is one in which Apple actually describes its customers. Moreover, it associates its customers with great historical figures idolised by many. It dares to posit that its customers share the traits of the greats.

You will notice that when these firms describe *what they do*, they do not focus on the product. Instead, they focus on the customer and why they do what they do.

In the article "Creating powerful competency models", Troels Dalgård and Esben Kristian Berg Jørgensen write that competency models help firms "translate their strategy into behaviour". They suggest that "successful strategy implementation comes down to people changing behaviour" (Dalgård and Jørgensen, 2016).

This behaviour informs the organisational culture outlined in Chapter Two.

So, using the Power of Three for sustainable competitive advantage to complete the model, you need to – according to

Dalgård and Jørgensen – firm up these three strategic elements, as shown in Figure 6, in order to outline the competency model:

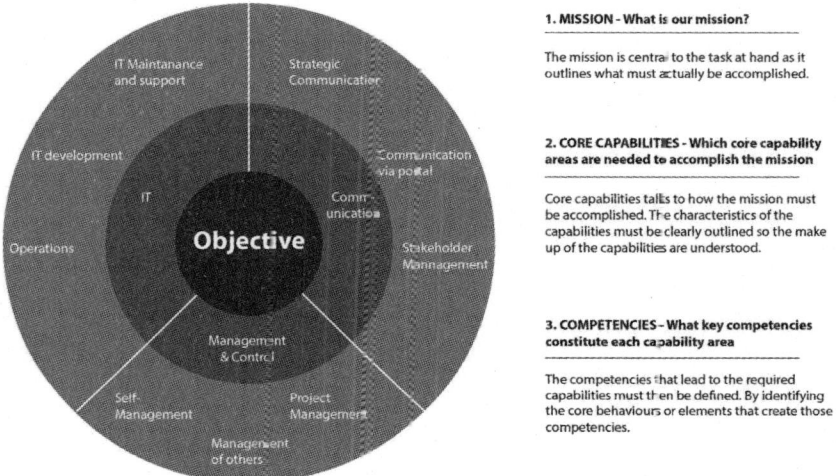

Figure 6: Competency Model with an example on an IT portal (Dalgård & Jørgensen, 2016)

In Figure 6, the Mission refers to the question, "*What* is it that you actually do?" Core Capabilities and Competencies point to: "*How* do you do what you do?". Once these are crystal clear as per the competency model, they will create a playbook of how you implement your strategy. This can inform how you manage change and how you recruit, train and manage to achieve your mission.

Consider the examples I've cited from Revlon, Amazon, Airbnb and Apple, and try applying the competency model to simplify what you actually do by putting the customer first. What you do must be stated as simply as possible, because "*when you simplify how you understand your business. You simplify how your customers see the value that you offer them.*"

5 Sell at the speed of currency

As an entrepreneur, you need to focus on creating value for your customers. Once the value has been created, you must focus on delivering it to the customer in the most effective, efficient manner possible. If sales are defined as "a trade of currency for value", then your entire organisation must be geared to effect this trade efficiently. Strive to create a sales culture rather than a product culture in your organisation. If you put the customer at the centre of everything you do, then it stands to reason that you should invest in constantly delivering value to the customer as conveniently as possible.

In my experience, the term "support function" is counter-productive. This applies equally to front office and back office. It immediately recuses itself from delighting the customer. This is because that support department thinks its job is merely to *support* the teams that delight the customer – and that they are not involved in doing so themselves. This creates silos in organisations and forms a malignant us-versus-them culture. It is the job of *everyone* in the business to deliver value to the customer in a way that delights the customer. It is that simple.

In an organisation, every conversation is a sales conversation. For example, the product team sells to sales and marketing what value their product or service offers. Human capital, or human resources, sells the organisation's skills that will be able to drive its value in the marketplace, and so forth. This is why every part of the organisation must be geared for profit. If it is not, then that part of the organisation is geared for loss, and must be either optimised or eliminated. If a division is not contributing to delivering value profitably, effectively and efficiently, it is working against the foundational principles and objectives of the firm. That division must then be optimised, replaced or shutdown – otherwise, it will cause organisational inertia, which is essentially resistance to change for the better.

Organising your company so that it focuses on delivering value efficiently requires you to "sell at the speed of currency". This means that if your service or product moves slower than the speed at which the customer is willing to pay for it, they will find someone else to provide that service or product. This is especially true in this age of instant gratification. Customers move for better and faster service.

However, on the issue of service versus price, Accenture reports that 66% of customers switch companies due to poor service. And, according to American Express, 58% of companies are willing to spend more with companies that provide excellent customer service. This implies that most customers would rather pay a premium for value delivered than save on value delivered poorly.

If you embrace selling at the speed of currency, you must prepare to disrupt. Embed superior customer experience in the value proposition or be disrupted. Deloitte (2013) reports that, "62% of customer service organisations view customer experience as a competitive differentiator".

Once you have your first minor success, start implementing rapid replication and proliferation, as described in Chapter Two. This is the path to your major successes.

Selling at the speed of currency means immediately embarking on optimised processes, automation and an enhanced customer experience. Superior customer experience must be part of the value proposition and the organisation's DNA from day one. The customer experience must constantly evolve, because it needs to keep up with customers' ever-changing demands. This involves embracing the latest digital technologies that will help you achieve agility, flexibility, scalability, accessibility and business learning.

It is time to consider sales at the speed of currency as a competitive advantage and to embrace technologies that enable this. Jia Wertz writes, in her 2018 article, "Why instant gratification is the one marketing tactic companies should focus on right now" (Wertz, 2018), that instant gratification has become "a basic expectation rather than the exception", thanks to hyper-connectedness and the age of the internet.

This connectedness means that we consume products, services, information, communication, work, social connections and entertainment digitally. This has been further propelled by the Covid-19 pandemic, which – for our own safety and that of our loved ones, colleagues and customers – has forced us to be more digital.

More and more companies are recognising the digital, connected environment as an opportunity. They are embracing it as a core competence and using it to deliver sales at the speed of currency – as a competitive advantage. Music-streaming services such as Spotify, Apple Music and YouTube Music are using the connected digital environment to deliver instant, on-demand music to subscribers for a nominal monthly fee. Video-streaming services such as Netflix, Amazon Prime Video, Apple TV, Showmax, YouTube and Disney+ also use this model.

Meals-on-demand service Uber Eats also embraces the connected world to deliver meals with speed – cheaply and simply. More than making life easy for the customer, Uber Eats has been a game changer for restaurants, making a business out of selling at the speed of currency. When looking at this through the lens of competitive advantage, you could consider that, in South Africa, Uber Eats is not the first mover in meal delivery. Mr Delivery was a phone-based meal delivery service before the company was acquired by Takealot in 2014. It embarked on its own journey to go digital and implement selling at the speed of currency, rebranding as Mr D.

A December 2019 Businesstech article documents Muir and Monde Masiko, head of product and user experience at Mr D, telling how they took the maverick start-up from analogue to digital.

Their goal was to get the order-to-door time to less than 40 minutes. They are now achieving an average time of 34 minutes! The article outlines five decisions that set the business on the path to selling at the speed of currency:

1. Mr D Food's CEO, Devin Sinclair, focused on an app-only strategy from the start. In 2015, no one else was doing this. It was a pivotal factor that led to our success. We leap-frogged past a traditional website to a totally mobile-centric strategy for customers, restaurants and drivers – betting that this would be the natural and best experience for our users in the future. We had to convince customers to migrate to and trust the app.

2. The group adopted the strategy of trying to be as agile and fast as possible. Time to market was key. Our competitors were close on our heels, so we needed to accelerate our roll-out. We used Amazon Web Services (AWS); 'going cloud' enabled us to have a solid infrastructure in place from day one. It was another pioneering decision in the context of the time.

3. Mr D emulated how Takealot deployed its infrastructure

using microservices to create a scalable business for the long term. It also made the critical decision to use Python – despite the fact that everyone was using Java. The productivity of Python 3 exceeds anything else and fits the Mr D iterative philosophy.

4. The business went with NoSQL rather than relational databases to further facilitate rapid acceleration without constant changes to the database structure.

5. The group built its business on iteration and data. Fail forwards fast – try it and see how customers respond. All our decisions are data-driven; everything is measurable. If you can't measure it, you can't manage it (Businesstech, 2020).

To help you set up your business for success and selling at the speed of currency – as done by the examples we've outlined here – Figure 7 looks at the building blocks of superior customer experience.

Putting the customer at the centre means that the three resources – people, process and systems – must work seamlessly together to offer a superior customer experience.

In this model, you need to give the customer the option of directly accessing process, systems and self-service. This also reduces your cost of sales or cost of service. To dial it up as a competitive advantage, you need to overlay it with customer journeys. Aim to build a customer journey map – a sequential graphical representation of the experience of interacting with your product or service from a customer's point of view.

Before you map out your customer journey, you need to profile your customer. Define your customer personas. This goes back to Chapter Four, where you define *Who is the customer?* Here you categorise customers into customer or buyer personas – types with detailed characteristics that represent sizable populations of your buyers.

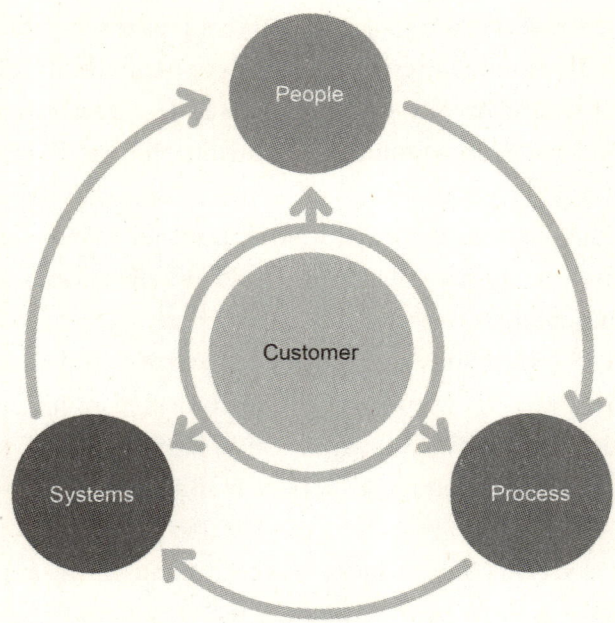

Figure 7: Putting the customer at the centre of superior customer experience

By clearly defining customers by traits and characteristics, you can largely anticipate why they buy, what they like to buy, at what price point and how they prefer to make their purchases.

This is all so that you can refine the customer journeys as you continue to study how their choices either validate or dispute components of these journeys. Figure 8 illustrates an example of a persona.

Defining personas and mapping out the appropriate customer journeys will help you understand how customers experience your business. This must include the customer journey when purchasing, and when asking for help. There is also a customer journey to renewing a service, upgrading a product or purchasing additional services. If yours is a subscription service, you must also map out a journey for when customers ask to leave you.

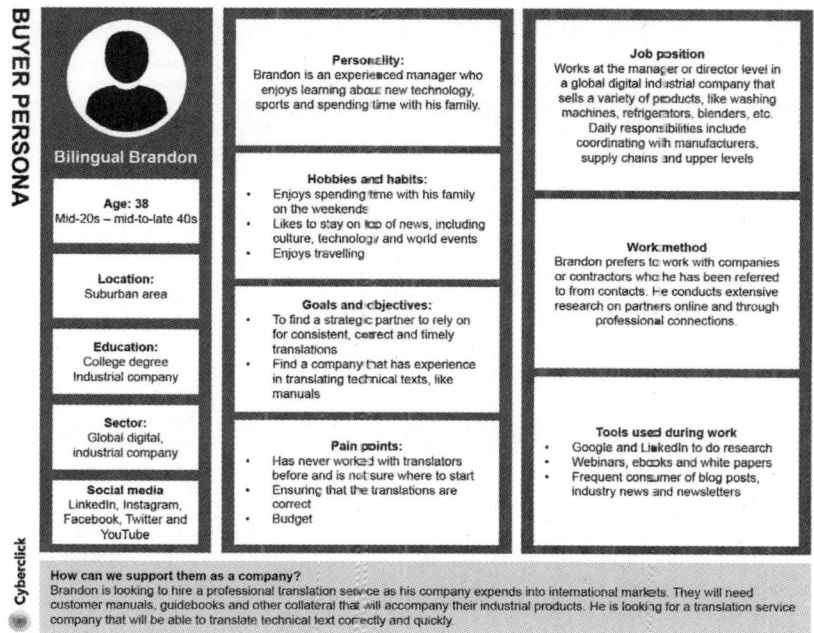

Figure 8: Example of a customer persona (Roberts, 2020)

I cannot stress enough that this must be from a customer's point of view, not yours!

Envisioning customer journeys helps you to spot any obstacles customers face when they engage with your value proposition or firm. After identifying the obstacles, you must try to remove them, along with anything that slows the process for the customer. These customer journeys must be regularly reviewed and refined so that they remain efficient and effective for the customer, eliminating unnecessary and wasteful steps. Lean Production, a concept from Japanese manufacturing made famous by Toyota, defines waste as anything that doesn't create value for the customer. Figure 9 is an example of a customer journey template you can use to map out your own customer journeys.

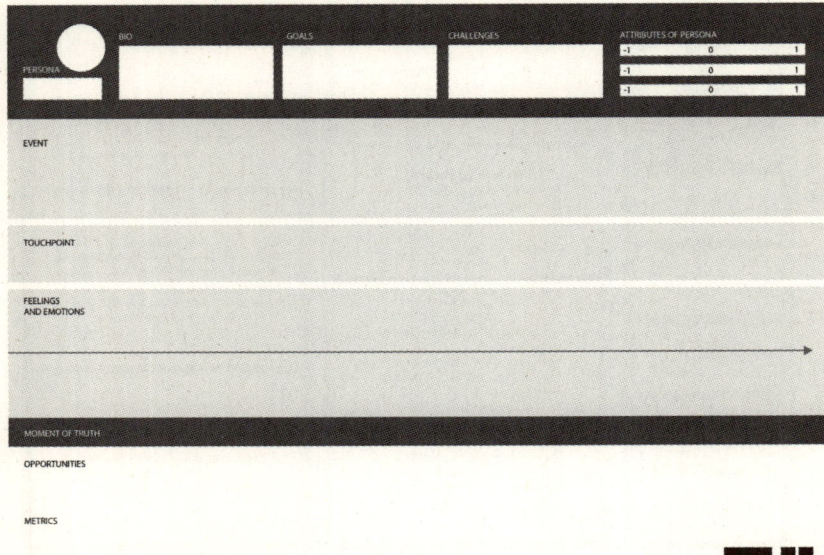

Figure 9: Customer journey template (Qualaroo, 2020)

Figure 10 is an example of a completed customer journey and all the relevant layers.

In a McKinsey article titled, "The role of customer care in a customer experience transformation", Stephanie Lotz, Julian Raabe and Stefan Roggenhofer write that "[the] process of mapping customer journeys is the only way to truly get a comprehensive view of the entire gamut of touch points and how they fit together" (Lotz, Raabe and Roggenhofer, 2018).

End-to-end customer journey mapping also helps to establish a single view of the customer, so that you can work to address all of the customer's needs at a single touchpoint, in what is known as a "first call' or "first click" resolution. The idea is to avoid the customer being transferred should they need help with another service or them having to repeat information they have already provided.

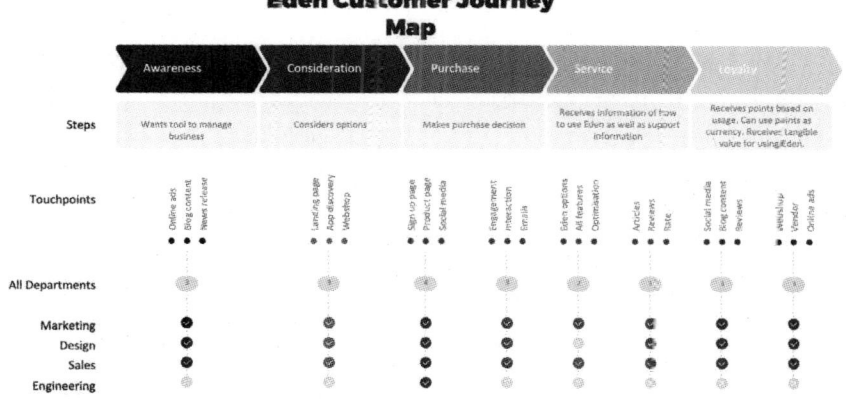

Figure 10: Example of a customer journey (Bright Vessel, 2021)

Lotz, Raabe and Roggenhofer suggest that there are six hallmarks of transforming customer experience and that the sequential application of these hallmarks helps generate and sustain superior customer experience.

Firstly, they state that organisations wanting superior customer experience need a clear value proposition. This must be followed by an in-depth understanding of what is important to the customer in terms of experience. If you've outlined your customer personas well, they suggest it's time to delve into the behavioural psychology elements in order to understand customer triggers and incorporate those into the design of your customer journeys.

Aim to reduce the number of things a customer must do to achieve the outcome they're looking for. By reducing the effort required from the customer, you're empowering the customer. To reinforce this further, you must also empower the channel, as well as frontline staff with all the process and digital tools needed to bring enhanced customer experience to your customers when they are not using self-service.

Look to establish a "listening" type of organisation. Constant feedback, surveys and assessments will show you ways to improve customer experience and your value proposition. Figure 11 is an illustration of how to apply the six hallmarks of customer experience transformation.

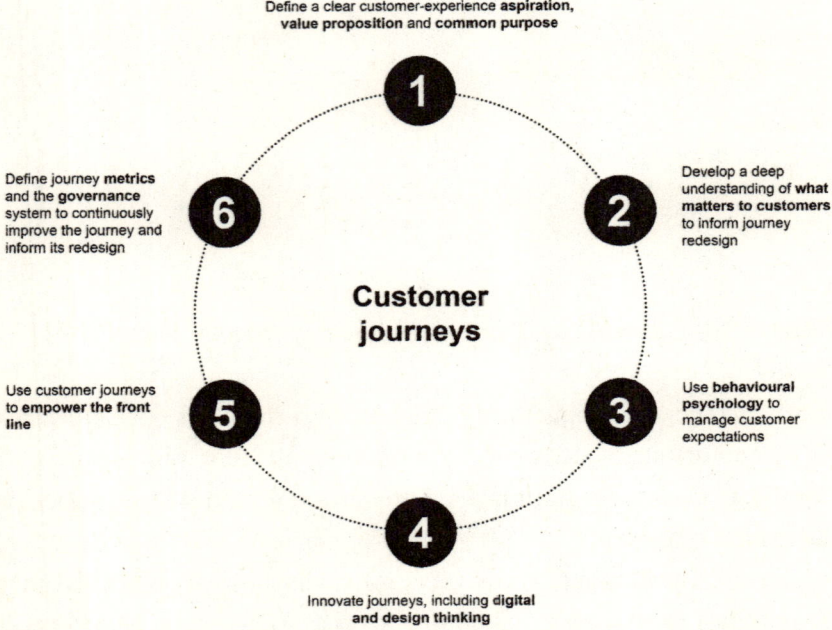

Figure 11: Six hallmarks of customer experience transformation (Lotz, Raabe & Roggenhofer, 2018)

Your customers need the value proposition at the speed of currency. If you fail to provide it at the requisite rate, someone else will. You will lose out on valuable sales.

Rather invest in honing your speed to market. Run fast ...

6 Run fast

You have taken your idea and implemented it, simplified the business model and accelerated your go-to-market model. Now it is time to enhance your business for optimal operations and success. It's time to put your business on a weighing scale to check whether it is overweight or underweight. This is where you determine how quickly your product or service finds its customers, while still maintaining quality and keeping costs low. Your organisation must be conditioned for business success in a similar way to how athletes condition their bodies for sports success.

Once you have embarked on Rapid Deployment and ventured into Rapid Replication and Proliferation, you are launching speedily to the customer, so as to determine what works and what doesn't. This empowers you to adapt quickly and eliminate or augment what doesn't work so that you can double down on what does. Learn to shed unnecessary weight without delay, so you can put on the muscle you need to succeed. This brings to mind the oxymoron that, "you must be selfish in your focus to delight your customer selflessly". In other words, you must not take on unnecessary weight or waste in your drive to serve your customers. Being able to adapt to your market and to sharpen your edge while remaining lean are strengths.

If you are lean and fit, then you can run fast. If you can run fast, that means you can outrun your competitors. This is why agility is a competitive advantage. Finance writer Caroline Banton says, "[E]fficiency signifies a peak level of performance that uses the least amount of inputs to achieve the highest amount of output" (Banton, 2020). In this context, agility is the business's ability to quickly and effectively adapt to market changes.

Building on the "Sell at the speed of currency" approach, as unpacked in the previous chapter, means operating at the speed of currency — in other words, your product or service must find the right customer, at the right time and in the most cost-effective manner, while maintaining high quality. Plus, you must be able to repeat this at scale, while enhancing customer value.

To sustain a competitive advantage over a long period, enterprises must move faster than the markets in which they operate. They must do this at the speed at which they make decisions and can implement them. We live in a fast-paced world, and the organisations that thrive are those that operate at the speed of currency — and can keep up when the speed of currency changes.

Change is the only constant. Customer needs remain the same, but how they consume what satisfies those needs changes rapidly. These changes come in waves, and your ability to navigate them will determine your competitiveness and continued relevance. Adapting to change requires reorganising quickly by modifying strategy, structure, processes, systems and people. There is no escaping this because it remains a business truth that what made you successful today will not necessarily serve you tomorrow. Evolving is fundamental to our very existence.

But you must also know how to change – and change well – because not all change is executed effectively. Running a successful business is about how you organise your internal strengths to respond to evolving external challenges and opportunities. How well you do this determines your sustainability.

The rate of change is accelerating rapidly, and disruptive trends are becoming more and more prevalent. Underpinning all of this is the digital revolution, as it transforms whole industries, markets, economies and even societies. The four trends that illustrate this are outlined by Wouter Aghina, Karin Ahlback, Aaron de Smet, Gerald Lackey, Michael Lurie, Monica Murarka and Christopher Handscomb in the 2018 McKinsey article, "The five trademarks of agile organizations".

> *i. Quickly evolving environment.* All stakeholders' demand patterns are evolving rapidly: customers, partners, and regulators have pressing needs; investors are demanding growth, which results in acquisitions and restructuring; and competitors and collaborators demand action to accommodate fast-changing priorities.
>
> *ii. Constant introduction of disruptive technology.* Established businesses and industries are being commoditised or replaced through digitisation, bioscience advancements, the innovative use of new models, and automation. Examples include developments such as machine learning, the Internet of Things, and robotics.
>
> *iii. Accelerating digitisation and democratisation of information.* The increased volume, transparency, and distribution of information require organisations to rapidly engage in multidirectional communication and complex collaboration with customers, partners, and colleagues.
>
> *iv. The new war for talent.* As creative knowledge- and learning-based tasks become more important, organisations need a distinctive value proposition to acquire – and retain – the best talent, which is often more diverse. These 'learning workers' often have more diverse origins, thoughts,

composition, and experience and may have different desires (for example, millennials) (Aghina et al., 2018).

These five trademarks of agile companies are great indicators of effectiveness, as outlined in Table 2.

Table 2: Five trademarks of agile companies (Aghina et al., 2018)

	Trademark	Organisational-agility practices[1]
Strategy	Single mission across entire organisation	• Shared purpose and vision • Sensing and seizing opportunities • Flexible resource allocation • Actionable strategic guidance
Structure	Network of empowered teams	• Clear, flat structure • Clear accountable roles • Hands-on governance • Robust communities of practice • Active partnerships and ecosystem • Open physical and virtual environment • Fit-for-purpose accountable cells
Process	Rapid decision and learning cycles	• Rapid iteration and experimentation • Standardized ways of working • Performance orientation • Information transparency • Continuous learning • Action-oriented decision making
People	Dynamic people model that ignites passion	• Cohesive community • Shared and servant leadership • Entrepreneurial drive • Role mobility
Technology	Next-generation enabling technology	• Evolving technology architecture, systems, and tools • Next-generation technology development and delivery practices

Data-driven decision making

You must first be a data-driven organisation, able to harness and learn from insights, in order to be agile. Keep a keen eye on market trends and organise your firm for adaptability. This means your organisation must be structurally flexible and not too hung up on siloed functions. The team must be cross-functional, with the strengths of each team member clearly understood. You can incorporate employee statistic cards – just as they do in some sports, with player cards. This will inform how you play to team members' strengths in different scenarios.

A change handbook

You will need to create a framework for change, which you can codify as a "change handbook". This would be a document that defines change in simple terms, but also outlines the levers of change and how to use them. It should also outline how to change and the rate of change to which your organisation subscribes. Your handbook should also outline a set of adaptive approaches your organisation can deploy in specific scenarios. For scenarios that have not been defined, the handbook should include a methodology of how to come up with the appropriate approach. Roles and responsibilities must be defined, along with the expected actions from each role player. Another important element that must be made clear is the reason for change. Knowing the reasons will help each role player play their part in realising the ideal change outcomes.

Change agents

Clearly define the characteristics of the change agents within your organisation. As a start-up, you can incorporate this profile into your recruitment process and so hire leaders who are proponents of change. If yours is a more established firm, you could identify the team members with these qualities and select them as the official change agents. When you have an opportunity, recruit new leaders with the characteristics you're looking for. An example of how to define the characteristics of change agents in your organisation is outlined in a 2019 Michigan State University article titled "Qualities of effective change agents", which are:

Flexibility: Being open to change requires an entrepreneurial attitude. Leaders have to tap into creative instincts to find non-traditional ways for a business to grow and exploit opportunities. This includes connecting with people of different generations and backgrounds to gain a deeper understanding of perspectives, experiences, and personalities.

Diversified knowledge: Successful leaders avoid getting stuck in the confines of their industry. By looking at what is going on in other sectors, and seeing what is working and applicable to their own industries, leaders can gain valuable insights and spot new opportunities for growth.

Priority and results focus: In creating change, it's often helpful to tie specific priorities to the overall business goals. These are must-win battles that determine success or failure and are focused on improving the company's performance in the marketplace. Doing this will streamline decision-making and create a clear picture of how the company is measuring up to expectations.

Ownership and responsibility: People respect courage and accountability. In order to lead effectively, executives and managers need to ultimately hold themselves responsible for their team's performance. They may have to make decisions that go against dissenting opinions and can cause conflicts, but doing so with conviction and ready to handle the consequences will ultimately demonstrate that their intentions are motivated by the best interests of the company, thus gaining the trust of their people.

Effective listening skills: Effective change agents are able to explore perspectives and take them into account when looking for solutions. This will help in getting buy-in to a change; people want to feel that others are listening to their ideas. Those who do will develop stronger relationships with their people by gaining trust (Michigan State University, 2019).

Key performance indicators

Set up clear indicators of success that you can reflect on daily. The change handbook must clearly describe what the triggers of change look like and how to respond to them. Clarify the outcomes you expect from the trigger responses. The outcomes could be key performance indicators (KPIs) such as net promoter score (NPS) – a measure of how likely a customer is to recommend your company, product or service that you can apply to any customer-facing element of your organisation.

Adaptive leadership style for change

Be a leader who adapts and responds appropriately to changing scenarios. Cohen and Tedesco (2009) suggest that leadership must be more adaptive, less accidental and less technical in order to maintain change and creativity. They argue that leadership for change should focus on the beliefs, attitudes and culture that support adaptive leadership. Leadership must also be an activity, as opposed to a position of formal authority. Bujak (1999) adds that leadership styles are important in complex, adaptive systems, where they must influence context and relationships to make positive changes.

Fenwick (2010) insists on a leadership/management dualism. He writes that *leadership* involves creativity, flexibility and conversations with all parties involved. By contrast, *management* is merely authoritative direction focused on hierarchy and administration.

Balogun and Hope Hailey (2004) categorise styles of change leadership in the following fashion:

> Education: this approach's aim is garnering support through educating the employees on the reasons for change and how, as well as campaigning for commitment and support.
>
> Collaboration: whereas the method of using collaboration

involves all the employees on the process of change, engaging them on what to change and how.

Participation: the approach of participation involves employees in some collaboration. An example is asking them for input on how to change but not what to change meaning that leadership still maintains control.

Direction: This approach is very authoritative, where leaders direct change by deciding what and how to change and delegate accordingly to the employees.

Coercion: The use of coercion is where power is used to impose change. This style doesn't take much input from other parties.

Out of these leadership for change styles, collaboration is more suited for complex adaptive systems. Bennet and Bennet (2003) suggest that collaboration plus increased freedom to self-organise means that everyone must be more aware of local situations, organisation objectives, vision, values and emergent activities.

Backstrom (2009) says transformational leadership with autonomy and integration creates a stable, decentralised resource generation environment. Silverthorne and Wang (2001) add that the more adaptive its leadership, the more productive an organisation will be. Johnson, Scholes, Johnson and Whittington (2011) echo this notion, suggesting that leaders and managers can harness innovation and new ideas by creating conditions that support them.

Hilburt-Davis (2000) adds that, "collaborations, with parameters, increase speed, flexibility, creativity and resilience".

As a leader, try to remove obstacles that hinder your teams. Outline clear, achievable goals. Create an environment of success, empowering your teams and team players, and managing the quality of inputs. My primary role as a leader is to remove big obstacles for the team and to empower them to remove obstacles themselves.

Revolutionary change versus evolutionary change

Implement incremental change daily. Instead of changing a lot all at once, change a little every day. This also means you're constantly redefining your competitive advantages.

Strategic fluidity – operating at the speed of currency

You must have a strategy, but you must also build flexibility and adaptability into your strategic framework.

> Distilled into its simplest form, strategy consists of creating a unique, valuable and defensible offer which addresses a significant target market. A unique offer is one that is differentiated from competitors' products and services in the relevant target market. A valuable offer addresses a clear customer need. A defensible offer is one whose competitive advantage is sustainable by virtue of the fit and alignment of the activities and capabilities deployed by the firm against the offer (Porter, 1996).

Jim Hatch and Jeffrey Zweig, in a 2001 *Ivey Business Journal* article titled "Strategic flexibility-the key to growth", suggest that the key to success lies in how well you recognise the need to adapt, understand how to effect that change, and are able to rapidly change at exactly the right time.

The idea is that your ability to effect strategic change is the culmination of a number of elements:

1. Don't be married to a concept
You must be focused on growing your business, and if your competitive position does not provide this opportunity, then you must be willing to shift focus.

2. Perpetually evaluate the competitive landscape

You must continually scan the environment for other opportunities – within your core business and outside of it. If a new opportunity comes along, position yourself to seize it.

3. Stay close to your customers

Be involved in the sales-and-service process. This will keep you close to customers' concerns and suggestions. Your ability to take the "pulse" of the customer and act on it quickly will be an advantage over larger organisations, with many layers between decision-makers and sales-and-service representatives. Use your smaller size as an advantage and create customer intimacy.

4. Stay close to your team

Communicate with your team regularly, at all levels of your organisation. Regular communication means ideas and concerns quickly become clear, so you can act on them sooner.

5. Maintain low or variable overheads

Organisations with many fixed assets are less able to adapt their competitive position. Minimise your overheads so you can readily scale up or down as required. This will allow you to modify and enhance your strategy and competitive position more readily.

6. Deploy adaptive systems

One Achilles heel of established organisations is their firmly rooted systems, which limit their strategic flexibility. Fixed systems and processes make it difficult for your organisation to change. This is largely because of the resistance of employees, who have a vested interest in the status quo. Small organisations are more likely to have team members with broader job descriptions, who operate in a more dynamic environment. Focus your teams on execution and encourage them to find creative solutions. Systems and processes must be adaptive, not hamstrung by rigidity in the organisation.

7. Fewer decision-makers at the top

The team must feel empowered to make decisions, rather than wait for others to decide. Better yet, these decisions should be quickly implementable. Have one person who will quality-check the decision and its outcomes. If the decisions turn out to be incorrect, ensure corrective action is rapidly taken, as per the change handbook.

Controls when operating at the speed of currency, and the communication model

Aim to develop a robust communication model to galvanise every single person in the organisation towards a single goal. You can apply Simons' Four Levers of Control to communicate and manage the outcomes of your "speed of currency" strategy. This will help you accomplish the following:

1. everyone in your organisation buying into the purpose and the change handbook;
2. managing your environment of success;
3. executing;
4. being organised for success tomorrow.

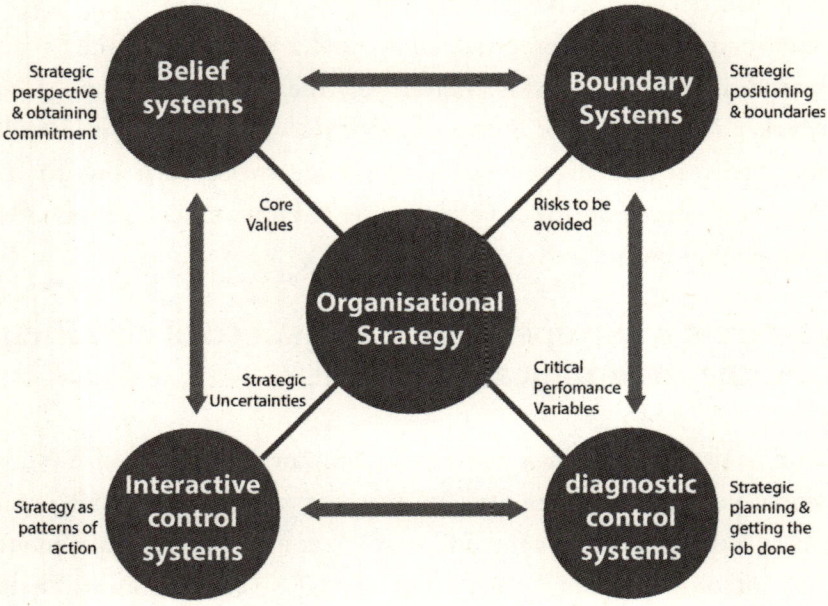

Figure 12: Simons's Four Levers of Control (Simons, 1994)

LEVER 1: Belief systems
What
A clear set of beliefs that define the fundamental values, purpose and direction of your organisation. These may include:
- Why you do what you do
- What you actually do.
- Most importantly they include why you do what you do.

Why
This paints the bigger picture, so that members of your organisation can affiliate to something much bigger. These could be outlined in:
- The mission statement
- The vision statement
- The team charter

LEVER 2: Boundary system
What

As the parameters in which your team must operate, the boundary system will have rules of engagement with defined penalties for deviations. This is where you define how much creative space you will allow; you do not want to stifle creativity with too much control.

Why

The idea is to create a space for individual creativity, where team members feel empowered, but with clear limits on where that freedom ends. The boundary system will include:
- Code of conduct
- Planning guidelines
- Framework for execution
- Procurement systems
- Operating model
- Call cycles

LEVER 3: Diagnostic control system
What

The diagnostic control system is your organisation's feedback loop. This is where you monitor progress towards your desired outcomes and make corrections if performance standards are not met. Corrective parameters should also be defined upfront. These will include:
- Key performance areas
- Key performance indicators
- Project milestones
- Organisational milestones

Why

The diagnostic control system will help:
- With efficiency, as well as resource planning and execution

- Set clear, achievable goals
- Apply relevant corrective measures
- Define outcomes-driven initiatives

LEVER 4: Interactive control system
What

This system is a management model you can use to administer strategic feedback, where new ideas in your organisation are considered. It can also use data and insights to foster business learning. Used correctly, these systems can perfectly position your company for the future.

Why

The interactive control system will help:
- Pick areas of focus in the context of changing market conditions
- Prioritise initiatives that will yield the best results the quickest
- Monitor the changes in customer patterns

Employing an interactive control system will ensure that data and market insights are factored into the strategy. These may include changes in technology and competitive landscape, or your own organisational strengths in relation to external challenges and opportunities. Constant communication and evaluation allows you to audit your strategy to ensure that it is still the most appropriate for success. It is important to always go back to the Power of Three and check this against the three questions:
- *Why* do you do what you do?
- *What* is it that you actually do?
- *How* do you do what you do?

Building a high-impact team (HIT)

You need a great team if you want to run fast – one that can adapt quickly to change. One of the best pieces of business advice I have ever received came after one of my failed entrepreneurial initiatives. "The right skills in the right functions pay for themselves," I was told. As a bootstrapping start-up entrepreneur, you are often tempted to fill several roles in your company, to do everything yourself. Unfortunately, this can lead to you filling roles you are not particularly good at, instead of recruiting people with the right skills.

Bringing in competent people to fill the appropriate roles gives a firm the capacity to be successful. But it doesn't end there. It is important to build a high-impact team. There's a team for every goal – this is why teams must be able to evolve as business objectives change.

Build your dream team. Focus on putting that team together, instead of creating hierarchies. In my organisation, I call this high-impact team the HIT Squad. It's best to keep this team small, but multitalented, with every team member bringing a unique quality to the collective. Another reason for keeping the team small is that large groups tend to lose focus and "social loafing" creeps in. As defined in 1913 by French agricultural engineering professor Max Ringelmann, social loafing is a phenomenon in which people working in large groups tend not to put in as much individual effort as they could. They feel their efforts will largely be drowned out by the rest of their team.

Joseph Folkman, in a 2016 *Forbes* article titled "5 ways to build a high-performance team", suggests there are five elements you need to implement in order to build your HIT Squad. He calls them "dimensions that deliver high performance", which are the following:

1. Inspire more than you drive

Learn how to create energy and enthusiasm in your HIT Squad. Help your team members feel inspired, as though they are on a mission and their role is of great importance.

2. Resolve conflicts and increase co-operation

Address team differences quickly and directly, but first you must establish a basis of trust and transparency. Remove any uncertainty that the flow of information is accurate, honest and inclusive. Once no one is worried about this, you have established a basis for deep, honest and meaningful conversations where differing views are welcome. You want to avoid a situation where team members' guards are up. This makes it difficult to communicate sincerely.

3. Set stretch goals

I remember vividly what my high school geography teacher, Ms Milton, told me 20 years ago. "If you're at a disadvantage and your starting point is behind that of your peers, then use that gap as a run-up. By the time you get to where they started, you will be faster and stronger than they are." That momentum will fuel success.

I have also learned in business that you must stretch yourself beyond guaranteed success. Aim for the moon! If you fail, you still land amongst the stars, they say. In other words, set aspirational targets. Such "stretch goals" create an impetus that can help the team achieve the impossible. The way I see it, if the team fails to meet the stretch goal, they will still land up on target.

Folkman says, "People don't really want to come to work and do something that any other team could accomplish; they want to do something extraordinary. When they accomplish something that is extraordinary they recognise that they personally are capable and competent. Doing something out of the ordinary helps people recognise that they are exceptional and their satisfaction with work, their engagement and pride all go up" (Folkman, 2016).

4. Communicate the vision and direction clearly and frequently

Stay on message, constantly communicating and keeping people single-mindedly focused on the vision and the mission. Use the Power of Three to summarise your message and use it at every opportunity when you address the team. It's your job to keep the teams informed, up to date and on track.

5. Establish trust in yourself

As a basis, you must have the trust of the team you lead. To do that, you must be willing to be vulnerable, to let your teams into what makes you tick, what your values are, and what you regard as success. Aim to connect with each team member according to his or her own qualities and not just as a collective. This is how you identify the strengths and weaknesses, the values and drivers, of each member. Try to find a connection point with each person and use that as a basis for your communication and guidance.

Adopt an adaptive leadership style that can adjust to any situation. This will help you approach every situation on its own merits, maintaining equanimity and an open mind. Leading can be most effective when we keep a balanced mental state, unswayed by preconceived ideas and emotions.

You are responsible for lives and livelihoods, so you need to build mental strength as a solid foundation to help you deal with your leadership challenges. But back that up by being sincere and dependable. Your team must know you will strive to make the right decision for the customer, for them, the firm, the community and society at large. Once you have chosen to lead, you must inhabit this responsibility completely. Trust is a cornerstone of high-impact teams.

Agility is key to winning and successfully navigating various market opportunities and challenges. The high-impact team needs to make agility a basic principle of everything it does. More importantly, it should be in the DNA of your entire organisation. Agility should characterise how initiatives are managed, how projects are run and how key performance indicators are monitored. The way teams execute their duties and hand over to the next team should be done with agility – efficiently, effectively and collaboratively, all for the sake of the mighty customer.

I use the term "mighty customer" because that is who you, as a business, exist for. In Rapid Deployment and Proliferation, the core objective is to rapidly generate value – in a delightful manner – to your customer. With this focus, you will not only stay ahead of your customers' needs and be able to service them, but will also help you succeed by staying ahead of competitors.

So, make running fast the basis of your competitive edge. At the same time, learn to run faster, so you can stay ahead of disruptive elements.

7 Run faster

Gear your organisation to run faster than its fiercest rivals. This means that innovation must be a daily activity rather than an afterthought. Innovation is the responsibility of every person in the organisation not just the founders or a separate department. The firm should never lose its entrepreneurial spirit, so it must embrace the "fail fast, fail forward" model. Never punish mistakes made in the process of innovating.

This is where Kaizen – the act of continuous improvement – must be ingrained in the psyche of your organisation, at all levels of operations.

A sure-fire way to run better and faster than competitors is to establish competitive advantages – as mentioned in previous chapters. In 2014, I wrote a paper called "Incumbents versus disruptive newcomers" in which I noted that, "without a sustainable competitive advantage, a company has limited reasons to exist". But, as I have mentioned, what makes you successful today is not what will make you successful tomorrow. Innovation is a key component of continued success and survival for your organisation. I must clarify here that innovation refers not only to product development, but to all ways of delivering value to the customer. Look to innovate in successfully delighting the customer, in whatever area you can.

The word "innovation" comes from the Latin word *innovare*, which means "to renew". It is the process of markedly improving value, service or process. It also refers to completely replacing any of those elements with distinctively better outcomes. You achieve those outcomes by having a clear picture of the end goal. You then constantly refine your existing methods, even using out-of-the-box applications. Ask, "If we do this completely differently, would it yield better results, more efficiently?" If the answer is yes, what does "different" look like?

Be bold enough to prove your concept. If it passes, you scale it up. If it doesn't work, then you learn from it. As a smaller firm, you may be wary of the cost of proving a concept versus the benefit of learning if it doesn't work.

Having started a company from scratch and grown it successfully, with many failures in between, my experience is that no effort goes to waste.

When trying something new, you should know what outcomes you want – whether it works the way you intended or not. Even failure is extremely useful if you know how to use it well. As I always say, how much you will succeed is directly proportional to how much you are willing to fail.

To embrace this notion, you have to know that failure is an important part of success. I would be so bold as to say that if you're not willing to embrace failure, you cannot innovate. This is where most established firms find themselves after they have established their winning formula. They tend to want to stick with that formula, even when data shows that its efficacy is waning as market conditions change. This is the point at which the risk of not changing outweighs the risk of changing, and the road to obsolescence begins. Competitors who are willing to try new things start to overtake them. Disruptive new market entrants start to nibble at their customer base. This is also the point where churn (loss of customers) becomes a problem. There are many cautionary tales.

It's easy to name organisations that have fallen prey to this and have been disrupted – Kodak, Nokia, MySpace, BlackBerry, for instance – and the internet is full of case studies written about them.

The approach I will take, however, is to share the signs of an entity that is ripe to be disrupted – an organisation that desperately needs to innovate and relook at its business model.

I have already mentioned a few of these signs: increasing churn; new entrants eroding your customer base; competitors adopting new methods and winning in parts of the market where you used to win. In a 2017 bizcommunity.com article titled "12 signs your business model may be broken", digital entrepreneur Matt Brown outlines indications that your business could be in trouble. He says these warning signs are usually there for about one to three years before the worst happens. Brown says to be on the lookout for the following:

1. Consistently declining revenues

You are no longer billing as much as you were. This should concern you, because revenue is a lag indicator driven by lead indicators such as new customer acquisition, churn and average revenue per user. More on this in the following chapter.

2. Sudden loss of market share

This implies that other players are eating away at your customer base.

3. Consistent loss of new business

An indication you are losing your competitive advantages. Other players are edging ahead of you, or the customer no longer feels compelled to buy from you. This is an opportunity to evaluate your value proposition and competitive advantages.

4. Disrupted by new competitors

New market entrants are one thing, but when they start to disrupt your business and steal your customers, that spells trouble.

5. Price points increase faster than inflation rate

When your cost of sales goes up and your profit margins thin out, that means your price points can no longer compete. This is especially challenging against new market entrants with lower costs, and established competitors refining their competitive advantages to remain lean. This is a sign you're no longer able to operate at the speed of currency and your efficiencies are broken.

6. No digital distribution channel

In a world where smartphone penetration is north of 90% and connectivity is on the up, a business without digital sales and service channels is essentially off the grid. Brown says that, in his experience, 30% to 80% of sales opportunities will be lost if you don't have any digital distribution and service channels. In one of the sales organisations that I have run, we increased sales by more than 60% by introducing digital channels.

7. No clear profit formula

This is the worst position you can find yourself in as an organisation. This is a mistake I made in the first two quarters of a successful start-up I founded when I was 23, but I was never clear on which product lines yielded the most profit and how. As much as I had a sense of the loss-making ones, I wasn't sure *how* they were making a loss. Ultimately, I had no clear formula for how to generate the profits needed to run a sustainable organisation. The result was that some months were good, and some months were bad. This is normal for a start-up – but it's not normal to have no idea how to change it.

8. Diminishing net-promoter score
A reducing NPS score – as defined in Chapter Six – is when your customers are telling you to do something and do it quickly. It is best to listen! Identify the areas they are telling you to improve and get to work making the necessary changes.

9. Inability to attract the best talent
Talented people want to work with the best teams. If your team is no longer seen as the best, the best talent in the market will not want to join your outfit. This is a troubling sign, because without talent you will be unable to establish high-impact teams, and this will negatively affect your competitive advantages.

10. Inability to leverage new technologies
It's possible to create so much complexity that your organisation's processes fail. If your firm is weighed down by legacy issues, change and adopting new technologies becomes difficult. You need to go back to simplicity, to focus on making it easy for your customers to buy from you. Ensure that it's easy for customers to stay with you and for staff to help them. Technology is a critical enabler of that. But technology evolves, so you need a mechanism of easily

adopting new technologies at the right time to maintain the ease of business.

11. Antiquated value exchange

Constantly evaluate your value proposition. When the price outweighs the value you provide, customers will shift to products where value outweighs price. Watch this closely. Products go through cycles, and often there is a point of parity where the price matches the value. By then, customers have already started finding alternatives. This is when disruptive new entrants come into their own. With their lower overheads, they can buy market share by offering more value at lower prices. They know that once they've built a customer base, they can upsell and cross-sell products and value-added service to boost revenue. They also count on the lifetime value of the customer and price increases further down the line.

12. Cost structures that do not enable scale

As mentioned previously, be careful of investing in fixed structures that lock in costs for long periods. When you need to change quickly, you may still be stuck paying for infrastructure. Rather invest in adaptive systems and cost structures that are more suited to scale.

You may notice that many companies show these signs. Sometimes, entire industries rest on their laurels, and so become easy targets for an agile company that comes in and disrupts. Ensure that you stay ahead of market inflection points by looking out for these signs.

You have essentially three options when it comes to transforming your organisation. The first is to stick to your guns and not change at all. This is the quickest way to disaster for your organisation. The second option is an evolutionary approach, where you continually refine efficiencies. This will sustain your competitive advantages, but you need to keep ahead of the rate of change in your business environment. Also, look out for revolutionary market entrants that could up-end your industry.

The third option is a revolutionary transformative approach. This is an immediate, pronounced and sometimes jarring change. It will typically require an entirely new business model, since revolutionary plans seldom fit existing business models.

The real choice is between options two and three, or a combination of both. Each has its pros and cons. Look to be the initiator of change, based on data and insights. Look for where your internal strengths respond to the changing external environment.

The type of change must be timeously planned and executed. You don't want to be *forced* to change. That means you're in reactive mode, behind the inflection point. Playing catch-up puts you at a disadvantage, because you may not have the data required to make the right decisions. Risk is also greater, because the propensity for error is higher. This type of change is corrective rather than transformative, and the cost of playing catch-up is higher than the cost of proactively transforming. Rather disrupt yourself than be disrupted by someone else.

Transforming the organisation and positioning it for growth will require you to take some risks, embrace a fail-forward approach and to navigate uncertainty.

When looking to innovate, define innovation in the context of your organisation. In one of the technology businesses I have led, we deployed a combination of incremental and disruptive innovation to achieve exponential growth. In daily sales operations, we used Kaizen, the Japanese business philosophy of continuous improvement. We classified this under incremental innovation. We defined a methodology for this innovation and empowered operational management to execute against this plan.

The operational teams deal with these processes daily, and know what works and what doesn't. It was the best decision to empower them to execute their ideas for improvements, then get out of the way. Of course, as leadership, we were there to offer support and guidance as required. The result was that our core business advanced because of many small changes and innovations that yielded improvements and enhanced customer experience. Our Rapid Response Team was born from these ideas.

The second category of innovation we implemented was Major Transformation Projects. For this, we appointed a Programme Manager for Transformation. Her role was to always be five steps ahead of the rest of the organisation. If our mandate was to deliver against the goals of today (business as usual), her directive was to build the capabilities to deliver tomorrow (major innovations). She would partner with agents of change in all the relevant departments to build our future capabilities.

Major Transformation Projects were always forward looking, scouring the market, analysing competitors and using data to assess internal strengths for opportunities and challenges. We were then able to implement major transformation projects with the support of all departments. Projects included new distribution channels, and creating a training curriculum for success across our entire team.

The projects also included fresh ways to delight our customers. This function helped refine our value proposition. Through data and analytics, we knew which channels were the most successful, and which products and services performed best in which channels. This informed how we set up and optimised new channels. We created a customised way-of-selling curriculum that won an international award. We optimised our customer experience by enhancing our customer on-boarding process. We also extensively expanded our distribution channels and optimised existing ones. We even tried channels within channels and other innovative distribution models. We significantly reduced churn and doubled our growth in new customers.

The third category of innovation is what I called "Big Bets".

These are the high-risk, high-reward initiatives. These sat with me, as the leader of the organisation. I would use data insights around macro-economic conditions, the industry, market trends and the competitive landscape, but I would also talk to customers every day. I particularly enjoyed speaking to irate customers, because they tell it exactly like it is. I used their feedback to outline what major improvements were needed – if the data showed the issues were widespread. I would continuously assess our existing competitive advantages while closely monitoring inflow (new customers), outflow (leaving customers) and average revenue per user (ARPU). More on this in the next chapter. These indicators tell you everything you need to know about what needs to be addressed.

In my strategy, I had five key pillars, which centred around the customer. These were fundamental for achieving exponential growth:

- Compelling value proposition
- Great customer experience
- The widest sales coverage and distribution model
- Targeted marketing
- High-performance culture

Whatever the data and insights told me, I would use these five principles to decide which Big Bets to invest in and implement. I also knew the strengths and the passions of my team members. I would kickstart each Big Bet as a start-up within the organisation and assign the best-suited team member to drive it as their own passion project. I would give them zero budget and ask them to find creative ways of resourcing and implementing their projects.

They showed incredible creativity, resourcefulness and determination. Remember, these "passion projects" had to be run over and above the unrelenting pressures of their official jobs. The reward was that if a Big Bet succeeded, they would have created their own promotion, and could set up their own teams to go forward. If a Big Bet did not succeed, the reward was experience and exposure.

These learnings were carried over to the next project, because we embraced failure as positive. Since we encouraged people to fail, they wore it like a badge of honour and felt encouraged to try more innovations. An outcome of failing a lot was that our rate of success increased. We would implement in sprints, iterating quickly. We would use what worked and discard what didn't. The values we collectively defined as an organisation were:

- We always challenge the status quo.
- We put our best foot forward in everything we do.
- We put teamwork above individual glory.
- We do everything for the success of the customer.
- We play to be number one. Nothing else will do.

Big Bets we successfully implemented included relaunching a failing business unit, rebranding it, renewing the value proposition, designing and rolling out an entirely new business model and a new go-to market model. This was supported by a new structure and currently it is one of the most successful business units in the company. It even promptly surpassed the performance of other more established business units. Of course, several Big Bets did not work out.

We came up with an innovative concept for a new digital value proposition. We just couldn't build it fast enough. One of our biggest competitors launched it and garnered more than half a million customers within a month. This underlined how a lack of agility can be a devastating competitive disadvantage.

The following are six steps to creating an innovation culture that will help you run faster than your competitors.

1. It starts with clear goals.
2. Then define the strategic pillars that will yield the goals and outcomes you aim to achieve.
3. Underpin these by collectively aligning your values to the

outcomes and the culture you want. We set out to create a high-performance culture fuelled by innovation.
4. Define your innovation categories and your organisation's innovation operating model.
5. Give your people an opportunity to create the future they want to be a part of. Let them lead. Give them support where they require it.
6. Then *get out of the way*.

Theodore Henderson, in his article "Why innovation is crucial to your organisation's long-term success", writes:

> When a company has an innovative culture, it'll grow easily, despite the fact that the creative process isn't always simple. Tried-and-tested methods may be reliable, but trying out new things is a worthwhile experiment (Henderson, 2017).

Henderson suggests that innovation should always be part of your business arsenal. Having an innovation culture means you have a uniquely creative way of solving problems – and that can generate efficiencies that save costs and time. It's a competitive edge that can help grow your firm.

Gordon Tredgold, founder and CEO of Leadership Principles, writes that besides growing, standing out from competitors and meeting customer needs, you want to attract the best talent. Creative, talented individuals prefer to work for innovative organisations. They need companies that empower them to exercise their creativity and their innovative talents.

A mistake that organisations make in times of crisis is to stop innovating. This has never been more acutely pronounced than at the peak of the Covid-19 pandemic. However, in a McKinsey report titled "Innovation in a Crisis: Why it is more critical than ever", Am, Furstenthal, Jorge and Roth (2020) write that "history suggests that companies that invest in innovation through a crisis outperform peers during the recovery", reporting that shows how organisations that innovate during a crisis outperform those that don't by 10%. Furthermore, they outperform the market by more than 30% post the crisis.

This further illustrates the importance of innovation as a strategic tool for navigating market uncertainty. In your drive to provide the best value to the customer, you need to "run faster" than the elements threatening your organisation. These threats can be external and internal.

Innovation is a vital part of growth. To use innovation as a growth strategy, the basic levers of growth need to be clearly identified. The next chapter explains how you can use levers of growth to develop your company.

8 Grow

You cannot grow what you cannot measure. Therefore, it is crucial to identify the levers of growth in the organisation. This determines which initiatives can achieve the desired growth objectives. The Power of Three is particularly applicable here. It outlines three levers of growth that can be applied to business-to-consumer (B2C), business-to-business (B2B) or hybrid businesses:

1. Increase inflow
Inflow is the flow of new business into the company. It includes new revenue from new customers and new business from existing customers. Inflow essentially grows revenue and market share.

2. Increase average revenue per user
This relates to wallet share. For example, if the company has budgeted R100 per employee for the services you provide, but you are billing an average of R25 per employee, you only have 25% of the wallet share. You are under-indexed.

3. Reduce outflow

Prevent or reduce customers or revenue leaving the company. Outflow is a natural part of any business, part of an evolving customer base. However, every organisation must make a concerted effort to contain it. Outflow must never surpass inflow, or your business enters a decline in earnings.

Fortunately, there are tried-and-tested ways to drive positive outcomes across all three growth levers.

A Malaysian proverb tells us that "before you can multiply, you must first learn to divide". I recommend creating a Growth Playbook to sketch the *what*, *how*, *when* and *how much*. The playbook should clearly outline your growth objectives. Then define the how, the methodology and initiatives that will achieve those objectives. It's also important to clearly communicate when these objectives must be accomplished. Lastly, outline exactly how the growth will be measured.

Crucially, your organisation must be structured for growth across all of its functions. The business is only as strong as its weakest link. Here are six key strategic pillars for driving aggressive growth. Each person in the business should know them. They must know their role in meeting the objectives of the business, as well as how that impacts others in the company and ultimately the customer. The pillars are:

1. What value do we provide?

The value proposition must be simple and well defined for the customer. If it's too complex for your salespeople to understand, they will not know how to sell it – and it will be even more confusing for the customer. You want the value proposition to sell itself. The Power of Three works well here. For example, you can have three primary products:

- small, medium and large, or
- entry-level, intermediate and advanced, or

- cheap, fair and expensive.

You can then help the customer to customise their own product or service using a series of bolt-ons or value-added services (VAS). With the right VAS bolt-ons, you can grow average revenue per user. The advantage for the customer is that this gives them the flexibility to create what's most valuable to them.

Data is key to growth, so use insights to track which product sells the most. Also check which combinations are the best movers, at which price points, and through which distribution channels. Which are most cost efficient for your various products and services? These insights will help you update your product or service portfolio. Data can also help you improve offerings that are not selling well. Additionally, it can identify the right channel for each product and service. This comes in handy when you define go-to-market strategies for new products.

2. Who are we providing it to?

Once your value proposition is clear, you must be equally clear about who you're providing it to. Segmentation is important to your targeting efforts and to retaining customers. You must know who they are, where they are, what they do and what inspires them to buy your product or service.

When organising your business around the customer, you need to understand your customer's decision-making process when buying your product or service. For example:

- The customer identifies a need.
- They gather information, investigating the best way to resolve that need. This could involve affordability (how much they're willing or able to pay) and mobility (how far they're willing or able to travel). The urgency of the need will also affect their decision. Who they are determines how they address their needs.
- The customer looks for the most convenient way to buy.

- This will be affected by where they are – at home, at work, at leisure or out running errands. Private consumers and businesses have different considerations. Serving your customer requires knowing how they move around.
- They will explore alternatives, weighing which fulfils their needs best.
- Having analysed the information and weighed the options, they make the decision to buy.
- Once the customer has bought, they weigh the results of their decision.

You need to know who your customer is, so you can position yourself favourably along the inflection points of their decision-making process.

This is where customer segmentation comes in. Segmentation involves aggregating your prospective customers into segments with common requirements. These are customers who follow the same purchase-decision process and respond similarly to your sales or marketing initiatives. Segmentation can help you target different types of customers, who view the value of your products and services in different ways.

Segmentation is important in tailoring stronger, more focused messaging to specific customers. Look to iterate until you identify the precise actions that yield the best outcomes. Knowing your customer also means you understand what works and what doesn't. You can use this to differentiate your positioning compared to your competitors. Look to create a two-way dialogue with your customers, where you communicate your messages and they provide feedback through their buying decisions and your digital communication channels. Iterate until you find the right messaging for the right channels and the right times.

Build your Growth Playbook based on your customer segmentation.

Analyse your customers. If you are a start-up or launching a new product, conduct focus groups with potential customers. Speak to groups of friendly customers that may include your friends and family. Interrogate them for honest feedback to find out whether the product or service addresses their needs. In this process, a "no" is more important than a "yes". But be sure to also get insights around what would convert that "no" to a "yes". Go ahead and find a paying customer. Sell the solution even if it has not been refined. This is how you get to know your customer and the value they need. They will co-create the solution they want – *with* you!

In business, "no" is one of the best tools for success. Failure is a guaranteed pathway to success. I believe rejection is a good thing. *Yes* is revenue today. *No* is information for revenue tomorrow.

After you have completed a thorough analysis of your customers – interviews, data analysis, focus groups, existing buyer data, for instance – extrapolate this information into buyer personas so you can define your ideal customer. Buyer personas were discussed in detail in Chapter Five.

Once you have analysed the customers and grouped them into buyer personas, outline their buying decision process. Define how you will position yourself for success in that process. This is where you create your competitive advantages, where you perform your initiatives better than your rivals.

All of this comes only with an extremely detailed knowledge of your customer and the segment/s in which you operate. Try to know more than your competitors – that includes knowing what other players are doing in those segments.

Knowing your customer is handy, because if you know what's important to them, you will learn how to deliver it better than anyone else. You can build that capacity, then go ahead and delight your customer, essentially blocking out any competition.

3. How do we get it to the customer?

Customers want immediate gratification, so make it easy for them to buy your product or service, and easy for you to sell it. It must also be easy for the customer to use the product or service, to get help when they need it, to renew and even to leave when they want. In this context, customer experience is a make-or-break competence.

The success of customer experience is not only in how well you define your customer journeys, but most importantly how well you implement them, measure their efficacy and evolve them as customer preferences change. Increasing inflow and reducing outflow depends on how well the customer experience is designed and applied.

Automating and optimising processes is key. Moving to a completely digital environment is hugely beneficial. It is not a coincidence that those companies that are born digital are the most successful today. They are agile, scalable and, most importantly, easily reachable via any connected device. The digital environment also gives the customer convenience and control, because they can largely manage their buying experience from the comfort of their homes or offices.

Relinquishing control also cuts your cost of sale or service. Lower costs of servicing your customer means you can reduce your price by going digital. This improves margins, and helps you compete effectively in the market.

4. How does a customer get it from us?

The customer must always have multiple options for how and where they can buy your product or service. Reach and accessibility are key. For example, if you have one store in one town, that means you primarily cater for customers in that locale. But if you have a national footprint, you cater for a wider group of people and your customer base must be bigger. However, even if you have a thousand stores throughout the country, that is essentially still one option for your customer – the store nearest them.

Expanding options for the customer means creating other channels – such as an online store. The importance of moving to a more digital distribution model has been highlighted by the Covid-19 pandemic. Today, entire value chains are being re-examined, from suppliers to retailers, to delivery partners. We will also see the service sector incorporating digital methods in the wake of changed ways of work due to the pandemic.

This is expanding channels for customers, who can now choose to buy at a brick-and-mortar store or online. Another channel might be a sales call centre – either inbound, where customers call to make purchases, or outbound, where agents call potential customers for sales, renewals or cross-selling opportunities.

Another channel is a reseller model, where a company partners with resellers in locations where they do not have a physical presence. The resellers can either apply a margin or be paid commission on sales they make.

There are many other types of channels that a business can deploy, but customer experience remains essential. If you deploy multiple channels, it's important that those channels talk to one another. A customer's journey may start online and be completed at a store, for example. You don't want your customer to have to start from scratch when they move to another channel.

Having a single view of the customer across all channels and departments is important to create ease for the customer, but also helps your organisation to service that customer.

Setting up channels requires a few basic elements that also help with defining a go-to-market strategy:

- There must be a clear channel strategy, where there is a channel for each customer and product.
- You must accomplish the desired customer experience at a channel level. This is where your customer journey mapping comes in, as explained in Chapter Five.
- The channel must be profitable and sustainable for all parties – customers, channel partners, product or service, as well as your organisation.
- Channel enablement must be in place, including marketing,

- support, training and funding to ensure the channel is sustainable and successful.
- The objectives and KPIs for each channel must be clear to channel partners, the team, yourself and the channel managers.
- Make sure you have a channel management team that knows the customer, the products/services, the channel, enablement and the levers of growth and success.
- Build strong compliance and governance mechanisms, and know how to enforce them.
- The channels must be geared for success, so you will need to reward success and non-performance. One commercial model is a basic-plus-commission model, which pays partners a basic fee and a commission on achievement of certain milestones. You can include a claw-back of the basic should certain milestones not be met. Another is a full-risk model, where the channel partner is paid only via percentage commission upon a completed sale. This requires an exciting product and a strong, experienced channel partner. Hybrid, or part-risk models combine elements of both channel models. Investigate which model/s are suitable for your organisation.
- You must have detailed, 360° business intelligence (BI), with reporting and analytics offering accurate, on-demand performance reports across all indicators. The BI must provide segment insights about your customers, and how their buying patterns are evolving over time. This will help you manage and grow revenue, and keep up with customers' evolving buying decisions.
- Evaluate channel effectiveness on a monthly basis. That way, you can continually optimise your channels for performance, efficiency and profitability.
- Implement what is known as a Resource-based Productivity Call Cycle and Sales Cadence. This involves noting the

inflow goal of the channel, then dividing that by the number of sales persons in the channel. This will tell you what each person needs to deliver in sales per month. Take this number, and divide it by the number of trading days in a month. (If your business doesn't trade on weekends, then a month typically has 21/22 trading days.) This will tell you how much each sales person needs to deliver per day. Divide that by the number of productive hours in a day – typically eight hours. This will give you a target of how much each individual must sell in an hour. Once you have this view, look at your current conversion ratio – the percentage of leads or pipeline that converts to sales. If you are a new firm without a historical view of this, you can use the standard "three times cover" formula. This means that to make R30 in sales, you need R90 in leads or pipeline. Apply this in your team KPIs. Work out how many leads each sales person needs in order to deliver the sales required. Then break up the pipeline/leads required into effort. For example, how many cold calls, meetings and other sales activities does each sales person need to do in order to build the requisite pipeline or leads.

To illustrate how to apply the Resource-based Productivity Call Cycle and Sales Cadence Model, we will create an example. Let's say your monthly target is to generate R10 000 and you have 10 sales people. Your product costs R10. In our example, there are three channels: Field Sales Channel, with five resources; a Telesales Channel with three; and a Digital Channel with two resources.

Table 3: Example – Resource-based Productivity Call Cycle and Sales Cadence

Channel	Resources	Required Productivity	Required Pipeline/ Leads	ARPU	Prospecting Calls	Meetings per day	Required Pipeline Conversion	Revenue
Field sales	5	155	465	R10,00	10	5	30%	R7 750,00
Tele sales	3	55	165	R10,00	15	0	30%	R1 650,00
Digital	2	55	165	R10,00	20	0	30%	R1 100,00
Total	10	1050	3150	R10,00	135	25	30%	R10 500,00

In the example in Table 3, you will notice that the Field Sales channel has a higher target. That is because it is a high-touch channel, which means a high rate of interacting with the end customer. This includes face-to-face meetings and typically longer sales cycles. This, therefore, provides an opportunity for bigger orders. Telesales is medium touch and qualifies as a volumes channel, with more prospecting and closing sales at volumes. Digital is a low-touch channel, requiring only light interaction with a customer. *Pipeline and leads* is set at three times cover, which means that for every sale, you need three leads. *Outline* clearly how many initiatives – prospecting calls and customer meetings – your people must drive to generate the requisite pipeline/leads. Then set the conversion target. You will notice that targets are also set at a slight stretch. You will need to include stretch in all of your targeting for the channel, because if you fail to meet the stretched target, you will most likely land on the budgeted target. A channel mix will vary from business to business, depending on preferred distribution based on product/service, price, customer and planned geographical coverage/reach, for instance.

5. How does the customer know about the value we provide, and how and where to get it?

In the same way that there are funnel and sales stages in B2B sales, there are marketing stages as well. For example, in sales the stages are as follows: lead (prospect), upside (highly probable), commit (guaranteed) and sale closed. In marketing, the stages are positioning, awareness and targeting (validation and relevance). In B2C, the customer follows a decision-making process, as defined earlier on in the chapter. Therefore, it is prudent that you align your marketing initiatives to the customer's decision-making process.

- You must be there when the customer identifies a need. This comes from knowing who your customer is, and working to be top of mind when the problem to your solution arises.
- This will require you to be present in areas where customers find information when they enter the information-gathering stage, investigating the best way to resolve their problem within the parameters of their means and preferences. Other customers' reviews also help here.
- Design your channels to efficiently deliver value and provide convenience to your customers. They will, however, serve no purpose if the customers do not know the channels exist and how to find them. So you will need to invest in educating your customers about where they can get the solution they require. Once they have identified the need and the possible solution, they will look for the most convenient way to procure it. This will include where to get it in relation to where they are – be it at home, at work, at leisure or out running errands.
- Spend time highlighting what differentiates your product or service at each of those marketing inflection points. This is so that, when customers weigh which alternative best addresses their need, within their buying parameters, yours stands out as the most attractive option.
- If you have done well with your positioning and messaging along the customer's buying decision process, then they will make a buying decision in your favour. They would have analysed the information and weighed their options. Your product or service would have come out on top because it

- solves the problem, they can afford it and they can easily buy it. Importantly, information about it is available, and in the language of the customer. This takes detailed customer understanding.
- Decisions increase in value once they are validated. Look to validate your customers' decision to buy your product or service. Once customers have bought, they weigh the results of their decision. Customer testimonials and other visible marketing efforts help with validating the customer's decision. Reward the customer for their decision in greater value than they anticipated, in superior customer experience. The great experience will win you a customer for life.

Marketing is what separates organisations playing to win and those that are playing to survive. In business, it is pointless being the world's best-kept secret.

Marketing is a conversation with your customer. As you know, there are good conversations and bad ones. When you walk into a room full of strangers and there are people you would like to talk to, you must break the ice and initiate a conversation. As the initiator of the conversation, you largely control how the conversation will go. The conversation must be of value, insightful, interesting, engaging, fun, and sometimes funny – and it should never be one way. A conversation is not only about speaking, but also about listening. One could even argue that listening is more important than speaking, because if you listen well you can respond with a relevant message.

The basic principle when having a conversation with your customers is that you see them, hear them, respect them, know them and give them the value they need, exactly when they need it. You must deliver it where – and how – they prefer it to be delivered. In your conversation, they must feel motivated by *why* you wanted to be there for them.

6. What must each person in the organisation do to make sure our value is received by our customers?

The importance of clearly defined roles and key performance indicators cannot be overstated. But the big picture of why you do what you do is the guiding star and must be reinforced regularly. The fuel for the outcomes you seek is the culture you create. This takes away the burden of making every decision. You create workspace magic when the culture supports your objectives and addresses the needs of the customer. When this is fuelled by purpose, then you create a purpose-driven environment that empowers at the same time as it rewards the individuals in it. Your people attach their own purpose to the organisation's purpose when they see it as vehicle to achieve their dreams and fulfil something greater than themselves. When that environment is created, it will build a flourishing team that is willing to go to the ends of the earth to fight for the cause.

For a leader, storytelling is a powerful tool for engaging, inspiring and organising teams towards a common goal. It can infuse such energy that all you have to do is get out of the way. Stories engage the team, inspire action and invoke a sense of belonging and purpose. Individuals make teams. Knowing the individuals equips you to know which of their attributes will contribute positively to the team and which will not. Then you can train the individual for the team that you build. In so doing, you can mould the team for the outcomes you're pursuing, combining individual strengths to achieve repeatable team competencies.

Placing the customer at the centre of your organisation will help your team realise that the definition of winning is customer satisfaction. Organise your team to play to their strengths in order to accomplish that. Then give them room to be creative in meeting that objective. Different types of growth require different strategies, so you must clearly outline this from the beginning of your growth journey.

Other models of growth are organic and inorganic growth.

Organic growth is achieved through your own organisation's activities – usually by increasing output and growing sales. This is typically done by optimising internal processes or new product launches. You measure this by comparing year-on-year revenues. Then there is acquisitive growth, which involves inorganic growth through mergers and acquisitions. You can use acquisitions to immediately increase earnings and grow market share. Acquisitive growth has its advantages, but the downside is that integrating two firms with different systems, technologies and ways of work brings complexities. Cisco Systems specialises in this type of growth. Cisco is a global leader in networking technology. The company was founded in 1984 in San Francisco and has grown through acquisitions. Recently, the firm has moved into emerging technologies such as cloud, Internet of Things, software and artificial intelligence (AI) using this strategy. Of their growth strategy the firm says:

> Cisco's growth strategy is based on identifying and driving market transitions. Corporate Development focuses on acquisitions that help Cisco capture these market transitions. Cisco segments acquisitions into three categories: market acceleration, market expansion and new market entry. The target companies might bring different types of assets to Cisco, including great talent and technology, mature products and solutions, or new go-to-market and business models. Cisco particularly seeks acquisitions with the potential to reach billion-dollar markets (Cisco, 2020).

Cisco believes integration is fundamental if you are to succeed with acquisitive strategy. The firm suggests that part of their success comes from "investing in dedicated integration resources" across the organisation at strategic and operational levels.

They suggest that your integration methodology and process should start at the very beginning and must be clearly defined in your acquisition strategy. You should pursue acquisition opportunities only when there is a strong business case, a common business and technological vision. "Compatibility of core values and culture foster an environment for success" (Cisco, 2020).

You will do well if you can organise your firm for compounding returns, as they lead to exponential growth.

As you grow an organisation, you encounter complexity. How you navigate this complexity determines whether you will enjoy success that is sustainable. This is where ease and simplicity must be highly intentional in your organisation. Simplicity underscores growth, whereas complexity is the enemy of growth. As such, you must structure your organisation for growth. Understand how to drive your internal levers of growth, but ensure that the context in which you're driving them is conducive to success – and by "context" I mean your business environment. The following chapter discusses how you can create an ecosystem of success.

9 Create an ecosystem of success

Success begets success. So look to create and foster an environment that nurtures success and creates more of it. This should include people and entities that are successful.

Values are the foundation of an ecosystem of success and high performance. My personal values are honesty, hard work, always striving to be the best, compassion and respect. What is most valuable in my life is: God, Family and Legacy.

These values extend to everything I do and underpin my drive for achieving excellence. They act as a foundation in the success I've been able to accomplish over the years. They are also the lens through which I see the world. Through this lens, I have been able to identify the key elements that need to work together to create an environment of success for entrepreneurs. I have been able to make this assessment following two decades of being passionately engaged in the world of entrepreneurship – as an entrepreneur and as an enabler of success in entrepreneurship.

In that time, I have observed businesses that have succeeded and others that have failed. With first-hand experience in both, patterns started to emerge of what generates success. One also starts to understand the environments that support success. There are six elements present in such environments, the building blocks that will give your entity the best chance at sustainable success.

1. Access to information – data and insights

When starting or growing an organisation, you need access to the correct information, so the right decisions and actions can be taken. For example, you need a detailed evaluation of the industry in which you would like to operate or grow your firm. This extends to an analysis of your target market. But you also need information about how to successfully navigate the challenges of starting or growing a business. You may also need access to research-specific technical aspects about your business.

A Deloitte report titled "The analytics advantage" states that data is an important aspect of decision-making. The report says 49% of companies claim that data insights help them make better decisions. Around 16% of firms say that analytics enables key strategic initiatives. Additionally, 10% say it helps them have improved relationships with customers and business partners, and 9% state that it gives them a good sense of their risk and better capability to react to market changes.

Matt Gavin, in a Harvard Business School article titled "Business Analytics: What it is and why it's important", reports that 60% of companies use data to drive process and cost efficiency. He further states that 57% of businesses use it to drive strategy and change – and 52% of organisations use it to track and enhance financial performance.

Gavin describes three methodologies of business analysis. The first is *descriptive*, which is the analysis of historical data to determine patterns and trends. The second is *predictive*, the interpretation of statistics to model future outcomes. The third, *prescriptive* analysis, is the process of using trials and other methods to identify which outcome will generate the best results in a specific scenario.

Used correctly, there are many benefits to data and business analytics. It can help you understand your market better, so you can refine your targeting and messaging, driving sales and revenue. Moreover, insights make for better decision-making. Their efficiencies can reduce costs and improve profitability. Insights keep you informed of emerging trends, opportunities and threats, helping you successfully navigate evolving market conditions.

2. The appropriate skills, talent, education and training
Your organisation needs the correct skills at each stage of its evolution. These competencies are an asset to the firm and must align to your strategic objectives. Invest in ongoing education and training so the skills can evolve at the same rate as the organisation's transformation.

3. Access to technology
Technology enables strategy. Used well, it can be a competitive advantage. Even most technology companies do not harness the *full* benefits of technology for their good or that of their customers. If you can figure out a way to harness technology in your organisation, you can gain an edge over your competitors.

Technology has moved beyond being considered a good-to-have, to being an absolute necessity. The Covid-19 pandemic has also acted as a catalyst in accelerating the adoption of technology for organisations. McKinsey & Company reports in a survey on "How Covid-19 has pushed companies over the technology tipping point – and transformed business forever" that "digital adoption has taken a quantum leap at both the organisational and industry levels" (LaBerge et al., 2020).

The survey explains that most organisations have realised

the importance of technology for achieving and sustaining competitiveness. You should not just view technology as a tool to achieve cost efficiencies, but adopt it as a crucial component of your core business.

Khalid Kark, Bill Briggs and John Tweardy, in the Deloitte article "Reimagining the role of technology", state that combining business and technology strategies will be the only way to generate sustainable value. They say combining these strategies will create "exponential" value for organisations. To this end they suggest that:

> As the pace, scale, and impact of technological innovation and disruption have exponentially escalated, technology has become a primary influence on business strategy, strategic choices, and value-creation models (Kark, Briggs and Tweardy, 2019).

They write that there are five technology-driven forces you need to consider when making strategic decisions about your organisation:

1. *Convergence*. Consider blending the physical and digital world to design your value-creation models. For example, automating your value chain.

2. *Data analytics and applied insights*. These are indispensable when making decisions so that your organisation can be adaptable, agile and ahead of disruption.

3. *Competing horizons*. You must manage the business of today, while building the capabilities that will secure the business of tomorrow. In other words, the decisions you make today influence the success you aim to achieve tomorrow.

4. *Empower your customers*. Utilise technology to better engage and serve customers and this will help yield growth in revenues.

5. *Speed to market*. This is where automation is

recommended. Automation of business processes can enhance efficiencies and productivity while reducing costs. It requires having a detailed understanding of your processes, then simplifying them and enabling them with technology. You want to make sure that your processes are simple, agile, flexible and scalable. Governance must be built into the processes, so they are self-governing. But build ways to enforce the governance.

Technology will play a crucial part in your organisation's success. Therefore, it must be part of your strategy from the outset, as it will also enable your competitiveness, scalability and growth.

4. A partner ecosystem
Establish capabilities that will enable you to consistently deliver great value to your customers, where you are the *best* at every part of your process. If there is a part where you are not the best, and it is impossible or too costly to build capability at that level, consider outsourcing that element to an organisation that *is* the best. You will still achieve the best outcome, faster and at a lower cost. Should that element be so important that you need to keep it in-house, you can learn from your outsourced partner, so you can lower the cost of production. Learn to partner for strength. Partnering also gives you access to skills you don't have, and helps you extend your market reach with firms that have captured pockets of the market you're interested in.

The other benefit of partnering is a pay-per-use model – a good way of keeping costs down for start-ups and small businesses. Having a partner with capacity where you do not will allow you to pay only for what you use and only when you need it. This means you do not have to carry the cost of that function within your organisation.

Pooling resources with other organisations allows you to focus on your core value, while the other partners help you with competitiveness. Selecting the correct partners is, however, essential to success. Establish a partner-vetting process and an efficient way to onboard partners contractually and commercially. Partnerships are just like any relationship – they need to be nurtured and managed. To protect all parties involved, your agreements must be detailed and clear. Compliance and governance must be clearly fleshed out and discussed so that lines don't become crossed. The steps of dispute management must also be clearly outlined.

It is also not unheard of for large companies to partner with smaller firms. If you stand out at what you do, organisations will want to work with you. In 2016, the Accenture Collaboration Index suggested that global economic output could increase by $1.5 trillion due to digital collaboration. In South Africa, GDP would grow by almost $12 billion – more than 3% growth.

In the digital economy, the agility and innovation of smaller enterprises can help larger entities. On the flipside, the resources and size of large organisations can help entrepreneurs and smaller companies with scale. Make sure that your value stands out, that your quality is unparalleled and your delivery is the best. Drive innovation and agility in a way that positions you for strategic partnership and growth.

The Accenture Index reports that 11% of large companies' total revenue is generated by collaborating with start-ups and entrepreneurs. It predicts that in five years 21% of large entities' total revenue will be generated by partnering with start-ups and entrepreneurs.

You can pursue a partnership in a variety of ways:

Consortium
A consortium is an assembly of two or more individuals, companies or governments working together to achieve a common goal. The entities with which you participate in a consortium will need to pool resources, but be responsible only for those responsibilities outlined in the consortium's agreement. Each entity under the

consortium should therefore remain independent in terms of their normal business operations and will have absolutely no say over another partner's business operations unrelated to the consortium.

Joint venture
A joint venture (JV) is a business arrangement in which two or more entities enter into an agreement to combine resources for the sake of achieving a specific task. This could be a new project or a specific business activity. The JV will act as its own entity, separate from the partner's other business interests. In a JV, you – along with the other partners – will be responsible for profits, losses and the costs associated with them.

Reseller partnership
In a reseller partnership, you take a complementary or supplementary value product or service from another entity and resell it with your own value proposition. This could be to enhance your own value proposition or sell the other value proposition as a value-add to your own product or service. You could do this for a value proposition that you are not in a position to recreate yourself, achieving speed to market at lower costs, with enhanced value. Most established firms with good value propositions have set reseller agreements and the commercial strength to support them.

Channel partnership
With a channel partnership, you sell on behalf of another entity using their value proposition and brand. In this arrangement, you can offer your resources and skills to sell on behalf of another entity. You sell their product as they sell it and under their brand. The end customer is none the wiser that you are another entity. In the agreement, you would have to align to KPIs set out by the entity on whose behalf you are selling. There would be commercial rewards should you achieve the KPIs and penalties should you not.

Channel partnerships could also be applied to other organisational functions outside of sales.

Referral partner
In a referral partnership, you can refer leads to another entity, under the agreement that should they convert into sales, a percentage of that sale would be awarded to you. This is the simplest of all partnership types, as it does not require a lot of resources or hard work. It does, however, require strong relationships with potential customers and the partner, so you can influence the outcome favourably.

Strategic partnership
A strategic partnership – sometimes called a strategic alliance – is a relationship formed to drive strategic outcomes for the parties involved. The entities enter into a mutually beneficial arrangement, but retain independence. You may use the agreement to grow revenues, enter new markets, enhance your product lines or develop a competitive advantage. The alliance must be mutually beneficial in that it must achieve the respective goals of all entities involved.

Public-private partnership
Public-private partnerships are collaborations between a government entity and a private-sector organisation. This type of partnership could be used to finance, build and operate projects such as public health initiatives, infrastructure projects or community development projects. When you finance a project through a public-private partnership, it can bring diverse, needed skills to make it a reality and also allow a project to be completed sooner.

Rhett Power, head coach at Power Coaching and Consulting, suggests that there are "four ways to build a successful partnership". Power says that, firstly, you must set clear, documented expectations around goals and responsibilities. Secondly, you must regard your partner as an integral part of your team. In other words, outcomes must be managed as if you were managing your own team to achieve the intended outcomes. Thirdly, give the partnership enough space to thrive. This means allowing team members enough room to innovate and employ new and creative value-generating methods. Lastly, transparency and honesty must be the foundation of the partnership. Make strengths and weaknesses known from the outset, and communicate clearly and honestly.

Partnerships – including partnering with your customers – can be a source of strength and lead to great success. Be open to partnerships in designing and executing your operating model.

5. Customers who are willing to provide honest feedback

Treat your customers as partners from the outset. This will form an all-important dialogue with them, and will help you refine your value proposition as well as the way in which you deliver it. Customers buy to solve a problem and they stay because of the value they continue to receive.

Gesina Gudehus-Wittern (2017) suggests that you start by understanding your customer in such a manner that you know what they are missing. Define a unique role that will fill that gap. Make yourself valuable to such an extent that you monopolise the problem that you solve for them.

6. Access to finance

As mentioned in Chapters Two and Three, you need to invest in yourself long before you ask anyone else to invest in you and your business. The viability of the business must demonstrate itself in tangible outcomes. You can successfully seek external sources of funding once you have exhausted all of your resources to get to whatever level of success that affords you.

It is unreasonable to ask someone else to invest when you have not. However, access to finance is important to a growing entity, allowing it to source the appropriate resources and skills. Secondly, it can help to drive the necessary marketing campaigns. Marketing is crucial to an organisation's growth and success. Thirdly, finance helps you to compete effectively with both small and larger organisations. Access to finance is an enabler that unlocks the next phase of your growth and success.

When these elements coexist, they create an ecosystem that provides the best chance of success. Your entity then becomes the remaining variable. This is when you need to define your own formula of success. Use these elements to create a sustainable success formula for your entity.

10 Solving for X: Defining your formula of success

Now that the tools of success have been outlined, how you use them will determine the ultimate outcome. Central to that success is *you*. But let's first define entrepreneurship. As an entrepreneur, or someone entrepreneurial, you are able to create or grow a business. You will bear most of the risks and enjoy most of the rewards. You will commonly be viewed as an innovator, a source of new ideas, goods, services and business procedures.

Entrepreneurs are responsible for a large proportion of the employment in an economy and typically contribute massively to the GDP. You will thus play a key role in the economy, using skills and initiative to anticipate needs and bring good, new ideas to the market. As an entrepreneur, you will garner success by taking on risks and applying your formula of success. You will be rewarded with profits, societal impact and continued growth opportunities. Entrepreneurs are found in all walks of life. Anyone who takes an idea and turns it into a return is an entrepreneur. Entrepreneurs are to be found in townships, rural areas, peri-urban and urban areas. They are in their own start-ups, in corporations working a side hustle, or using their enterprising skills to help grow those organisations.

As an entrepreneur, you must have a clear vision, map out a clear path and work hard to realise it.

Where your passion collides with your purpose is where you will find happiness and fulfilment, while having greater societal impact than just for yourself. Mahatma Gandhi emphasised this notion when he said, "The best way to find yourself is to lose yourself in the service of others." In business, for you to succeed, you need a third element: the yield-return lever – in other words, "How can I present my passion and purpose to the world in a way that produces a meaningful return?" The yield-return lever differs for all of us; it's what makes you happy and fulfilled. This is why it's not advisable to copy other people's goals or outcomes, and why it's often said that "money will not bring you happiness". If money is not your yield-return lever, it will certainly not lead to fulfilment.

Therefore, the formula of success is:

(Purpose + Passion) x Yield - return Lever = Success

I have learned that the path to success is not linear, and the outcome is subjective. As such, no one should pass judgement on what success means to someone else.

This realisation of mine comes from retrospection. They say that hindsight is 20/20 and let me take you back to my formative years.

In my youth, I had ambition. The dreams and the goals were clear and the willingness to work hard was there, but the path to achieving those goals was not quite as clear. And so I followed what I thought was a linear path to success. I thought, if I worked hard at school, then chose a path based on what I was good at, I would subsequently land a job. Then, I would work hard to climb the corporate ladder, eventually rising to what I thought was the pinnacle of success. My rise would be accompanied by the perks of that ascent, such as a high salary, benefits and other material things. In retrospect, my journey to success wasn't so simple or as linear. But my purpose was staring me in the face all along – and I almost missed it completely! Growing up, we would wake up at 4 am every morning to either tend to cattle or to work the corn fields that we would harvest in autumn. At harvest time, we would have a feast in celebration of the yield. As a herd boy, I would also be rewarded with a big bowl of umthwibi – dry pap and the first creamy milk, produced if you successfully guide a cow in birthing a healthy calf. Our culture instilled the value of hard work in me. On Wednesdays, we would take the cattle to the dip before school. Working together to get all the cattle through the dip quickly taught us the value of being organised – you would get into trouble if you were late for the first class! In spring, we would strap up the oxen and use them to plough the fields, so we could sow the land.

I derived many lessons about life and business from this boyhood work. For instance, I learned that the hard work you put in during summer will set you up for winter. The best lesson I learned was that even though we were not the wealthiest in terms of money in the bank, we made the best of what we had. This is also where I learned my sales skills, because we would sell the surplus harvest. Simply put, do the best with what you have to get what you don't have.

This is why, at the age of 15, I embarked on my first entrepreneurial venture. Later, at university, I would sell mobile phones. Back when these devices were out of reach for many people, I would offer creative ways for customers to finance them. Since my monthly allowance was not enough to cover my basic needs, I would use the profits of these sales to plug the gaps.

I thought of these small businesses as merely a means to an end, something I needed to do because I had to. I was sometimes embarrassed about these minor and apparently frivolous ventures, because I thought I would be regarded as poor. Being poor was something I never associated with myself, even though I really struggled to make ends meet at university. Then I realised that business was something I was naturally talented at. Let me qualify that … I realised that I am naturally talented at understanding the drivers and mechanics of business and sales.

I have gone on to build businesses, successful sales organisations and channels that continue to thrive today. As a result, I have mentored and helped hundreds of people to create their own successes. This came from working hard as a boy and learning the ins and outs of doing business from people who did not go to business school.

The models I learned and formulated back then were validated when I went to business school, and some are models that are not even modelled yet. My knowledge came from doing what I thought I had to do to survive. Only later did I realise this was something I wanted to do, that I thrive in doing. And that, yes, without it I probably wouldn't survive. I am always mindful that using my talents to sell touches millions of people positively every single day. I also continue to share my knowledge, experience and understanding of how to harness one's talents.

In doing so, I am happy and grateful to have found where my passion collides with my purpose, and that that provides a meaningful return. Creating a cycle of sustainability means that I can continue to passionately live out my purpose in a way that makes the world a better place.

According to Karl Moore, author of *The Great Power of Connecting Passion with Purpose*, embarking on the journey to finding your purpose starts with three basic questions:

1. How have your passion and interests evolved to shape your purpose? How do they connect to your interests and dreams from your early days?
2. What pursuits would inspire and give meaning to you?
3 What impact would you like to make on others?

Moore cites T.D. Jakes, who explains it perfectly when he says, "If you can't figure out your purpose, figure out your passion. For your passion will lead you right into your purpose." Passion is what drives you. It inspires you to go that extra mile. I find that it also helps me focus on what is important. I can shut out anything that saps energy from what I am trying to accomplish.

Moore adds that you should evaluate your situation today against finding the purpose that will fulfil your goals of making an impact. To do this, you must work through the Four Ss.

- *Struggle:* Is your life a challenge, with significant risks in meeting your needs?
- *Survival:* Is the role that you currently play just for your security and to pay the bills?
- *Success:* Does the role that you currently play tap into your talent? Does it add personal value by achieving or over-achieving your goals?
- *Significance:* Are you creating excellence? Are you committed to a purpose that is bigger than you and about impacting others?"

The Japanese use the word *ikigai*, which roughly translates to "reason for being". And reason for being (or purpose) is where passion meets what you are good at, along with what the world needs and what it is willing to pay for. Figure 13 is the first exercise that I conduct with every single person I mentor. I would recommend that you also use it to find your reason for being.

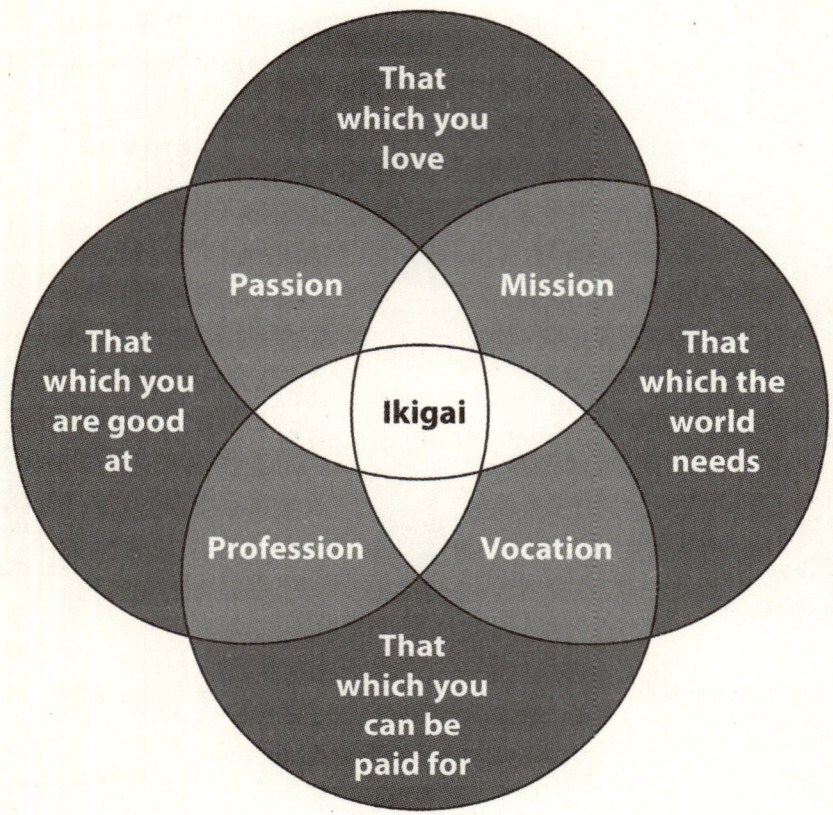

Figure 13: Ikigai *(The Institute of You / Mindfulness for you, 2021)*

Your life will find meaning when you identify your purpose – and it is fuelled by passion! On the path to finding your purpose and success, you should not avoid failure. Instead, lean on failure as an instrument of success. I have harnessed the lessons I have learned from failure in order to find success. I view adversity as a stepping stone towards wisdom and success. This approach has yielded all of my successes. After the catastrophic failure of my first business, I had to learn how to fail well, and that meant learning that failure is actually not the end, but the beginning of success.

The journey

Having lost all my money, I had to start my journey to success with nothing but the experience of running a failed enterprise. What I did not know at the time was that this failure would be the jet fuel to my success. I went back to the drawing board, and decided to learn from the mistakes I had made in my failed business and extract the formula of success. I took the long route. I knew that for me to get it right, there could be no short cut.

The marketing lessons

I went back to school to study postgraduate marketing at one of the best business schools in the country. There, I gathered insights and learned how to master segmentation and how to create and position value propositions. I also learned to be creative with marketing, communications and public relations without necessarily relying on a big budget. I came to understand that marketing is about engaging customers. This is when I truly began to love customers.

I learned that what underpins a successful marketing campaign is a robust sales-converting plan. If marketing proposes the product or solution, then it must create the ability to convert the sale. I have used this idea to delight the customer at every opportunity. When dealing with irate customers, the challenge of changing their experience from bad to great is an opportunity. It's another touch point, another opportunity to grow customers' commitment to your company and increase their spend. Every customer engagement is a chance to make a sale.

Mastering sales

I took a sales job in one of the best organisations in the world, and I treated it like a university campus. I would learn the mechanics of the organisation as if I was at school. I would apply what I learned, fail, iterate, try again, succeed, scale and repeat. As a result, I grew my knowledge. I worked in many roles and regions, all while mastering the craft of sales and building successful, sustainable sales channels in various markets. This gave me the opportunity of leading a multichannel, multicultural, multilingual team across multiple countries and markets. I had the privilege of leading a turnaround of a non-performing team into a high-performing team by applying the knowledge I'd gathered learning, failing, iterating, trying again, succeeding, scaling and repeating. We doubled the revenue of that project. It was validation that this model was working, but my education was not done.

Mastering business
To challenge and educate myself further, I enrolled for an MBA in International Business at one of the top business schools in the world. I learned all the facets of business. I learned that no business succeeds without a business model.

I acquired other business tools, but most importantly, I learned how to create a tool to solve any business problem. The highlight is that now I have lifelong friends all over the world I can call upon when I visit or do business in those countries. Some I call for valuable advice on business in my own country.

In the last semester of my MBA studies, an opportunity led me to start a consulting firm focusing on project management. My first project was a massive one, covering the whole of EMEAR (Europe, the Middle East, Africa and Russia) for an international firm. This is where I learned how to deliver quality outcomes for a big project while remaining lean and keeping overheads low.

Following my passion
Having started my career as an entrepreneur, I am passionate about businesses and what makes them successful. I'm interested in the components that lead to success, as well as the environment that is conducive to sustainable ventures and business growth levers. I endeavoured to create that for entrepreneurs in my country by

joining the biggest telecommunications firm in Africa and the Middle East. There, I led the Small Medium Enterprise business segment. As I had with other projects, I approached this in four ways:
1. To create value and technology that enables the sustainable growth of small enterprises
2. To find solutions to difficult problems through innovation
3. To build multiple channels to deliver the value to all small businesses in all corners of the country
4. To learn and grow, using this opportunity as a university campus.

To achieve this, I had to create a "fail fast, fail forward" culture in the team. In the beginning, I had a team of only five to deliver 70% of the organisation's budget. The ability to deliver massive value with limited resources came in handy. By the time I felt that my job was suitably done, we had grown the business massively and the team was 500 strong, having expanded reach and coverage through channel expansion and partnerships. But the impact we made for small businesses was even greater and continues today.

Pursuing my purpose
Growing firms and seeing entrepreneurs and their businesses thrive are actualisations driven by my purpose. Most people can relate to entrepreneurship, because most of us have an inkling to pursue it – or at least be inspired by those bold enough to do it and succeed. This is why I have distilled 24 years of learning, failing, iterating, trying again, succeeding, scaling and repeating into this playbook.

Eden
In the spirit of creating an ecosystem of success, as outlined in Chapter Nine, is Eden – a digital platform that helps entrepreneurs and small businesses manage and grow their businesses. The concept of Eden is based on the butterfly effect, in the belief that simplifying business digitally can achieve massive results.

Eden provides digital resources to manage critical small-firm functions, such as sales, billing, logistics, customer support and marketing. It also gives entrepreneurs and businesses access to a community of likeminded people and an opportunity to form partnerships or source goods. The digital ecosystem also gives users control of their business processes.

Aims of the Eden Portal
- To provide a tool that will automate and digitise critical business processes
- To provide end-to-end control and visibility to the business owner
- To provide live reports on business performance against KPIs and benchmark against industry and market.

Audience
- Eden is for entrepreneurs and small business owners – organisations that employ 1–199 employees.
- Eden works best for organisations that sell services or goods.
- Eden is useful for companies that need to manage and expand their sales channels.
- It is for firms that need to quote and invoice customers.
- It suits organisations that may need to manage and bill a base of customers.
- It is useful for small businesses that have suppliers, where they may need to collect inventory and/or dispatch goods to their customers.
- It works for businesses that provide services to their customers, whom they need to support.
- It will benefit start-ups that need access to relevant business courses and training.
- Eden will also aid businesses that need to benchmark themselves against their respective industries and see how

- their competitors are performing.
- It will also come in handy for the entrepreneur who is looking for a virtual assistant.

Long-term vision
- Eden's purpose is to create sustainability and growth for small businesses. The long-term vision is to have a majority of small businesses in the continent using the digital ecosystem to manage and grow their businesses.
- The digital ecosystem is easily accessible in terms of price. It is seamless, easy and fun to use. It also has a clean, simple interface.

I am fortunate to have found where my passion collides with my purpose. I am passionate about business and what makes organisations successful. My purpose is to help you and other entrepreneurs find theirs. My yield-return lever is "growth". In short, I grow things and get paid for it. In a similar way to how my grandparents used to grow crops and sell the surplus or raise cattle, multiply and trade, I raise and grow businesses.

I have practise in growing firms and, because I love driving that growth process, it does not seem like work at all. The actual execution is even more fun. I am passionate about seeing organisations grow sustainably and following the journey from failure to success. Not because there are no challenges, but because failure is an instrument of success. In this process you can even use challenges as validation that you're on the right course. In fact, over time I have learned to be suspicious of a path with no challenges. That stems from my experience that what was worth pursuing, always required a worthy fight. As such I always take the path of most resistance, because if the other paths do not challenge they will most likely not bring growth. I take personal pleasure in achieving an outcome that seemed impossible to achieve. Triumph against all odds.

Try to find your yield-return lever. Getting paid for doing what you're passionate about is rewarding. It must also be something for which you have reached a high level of excellence or for which you are willing to invest time and sacrifice in order to achieve that excellence. And, of course, if you love doing something, it never feels like work. This is the type of work that Mark Twain was describing when he said, "Find a job you enjoy doing, and you will never have to work a day in your life."

But combining passion, excellence and love is still centred around you. And that is not enough. The customer must be central to everything you do. Your passion, excellence and love must be useful. Combine your passion and what you are good at with something useful to the world – that is where you will find your yield-return lever or reason for being.

Having defined your formula of success, you must identify the point of success where you will exit. Much like you might enter a building and check where the exit is, you must know at which point you will exit your business. Done successfully, it will determine your profits upon exit. It is also important to define the point of exit if the business is unsuccessful, so as to limit your losses. Plan and prepare your exit well.

11 Exit

Planning your exit means you determine how well your departure goes, instead of external factors or other people doing it for you. The work that allows you to sell your business at the right multiple starts from the outset. It comes down to the business model you have chosen as your foundation.

Your business model

Jim Scheckser, CEO of the Inc. CEO Project, says the better your business model, the more valuable your business will be. In a 2020 article, he suggested nine questions to test if you have a solid business model or not.

1. Is the market big enough?
Is the market big enough to accommodate massive growth? Playing in a small market limits the size your organisation can ever possibly grow to. Popular wisdom holds that the size of a

goldfish is determined by the size of the body of water in which it lives. It remains small in a fish bowl, but can get much bigger in a pond. Not having a large market for your firm to grow into reduces your prospect of a buyer. A buyer seldom acquires a firm for it to remain stagnant or decline.

2. Is the market growing?
A shrinking market is an early indicator that customers have moved on and you're behind the change curve. This is a risk to your firm. A market that supports exponential growth should itself be showing double-digit growth.

3. What is your market share?
The ideal market share sits around 20% to 40%, as this allows room for further growth. In this range, you are best placed to disrupt and take market share from other players. If your market share is more than 40%, you should plan to diversify into even bigger markets. There you can use your strengths to grow exponentially.

4. Is the basis for competition clear?
As detailed in Chapter Four, competitive advantages are essential to your success. Therefore, your competitive advantage must be both clear and sustainable. It must be the basis of your future growth. Having a clear competitive advantage will enhance the value of your organisation.

5. What is the nature and percentage of your recurring revenue?
This is a critical factor when evaluating an organisation, because the more annuity revenue – otherwise known as recurring revenue – an organisation has, the more valuable it becomes. Annuity/recurring revenue is typically supported by existing contracts that result in revenue that flows into the organisation at regular intervals usually monthly – in other words, subscription revenue.

Moreover, the longer the contracts for that revenue, the better. Do you have three-year, five-year, ten-year or even longer contracts?

Work to get your organisation to where at least 90% of revenue is recurring revenue. You will be able to use this as a baseline for growth, instead of spending time chasing the next non-recurring order. Think of it this way: it takes just as much effort to chase business that will pay you monthly for 10 years as it does to get business that only pays for one month.

Why would you spend all of that energy for a single payment? Even more so on a model where you have to repeat that effort every single month? Recurring revenue means you can focus your energies on retaining the customer and initiatives to grow the recurring revenue even further.

6. What is your annual customer retention percentage?

Inflow and outflow are two sides of the same coin when we talk about recurring revenue. In an ideal world, you would retain 100% of your customer base. But the reality is that churn, or outflow, is a part of any business with a recurring-revenue customer base.

Your job is to retain at least 95% of that base going into every new year by making sure those customers are in-contract, engaged and satisfied. In-contract means, for example, that if the customer had originally signed up for a 36-month contract, between month 1 and month 36 they are in-contract. But from month 37 they are out-of-contract even though you may still be providing them the service. The objective is to keep your customers in-contract, because the likelihood for a customer to cancel the contract is much higher when they are out-of-contract. You will thus need to renew the contract when the customers' contracts come to term. Additionally, you can enrich revenue through upselling and cross-selling into that base. Establish this as a crucial competence in your organisation. You must also offset outflow by accelerating inflow. Ultimately, the aim is to never lose more than 5% of your customer base in a financial year. To offset that, you must also never grow at less than 10% annually. That's just your baseline growth – your growth target is over and above that.

7. What is your gross margin?

Scheckser says, "[Gross] margin is your net income after accounting for cost of goods sold, but before you take out your overhead expenses. A good gross margin is around 80 to 90%. That's when you're creating cash, and cash creates opportunities to grow. If your gross margin is at the other end of the spectrum – 15% or lower – your business will be considerably less valuable."

8. How capital intensive is your business?

Build a business model where you do not need much capital to deliver your value to your customers. It is difficult to create shareholder value in a capital-intensive business, because it is difficult to get money out. If your capital is tied up in operations, you can't invest in developing your business. If your cash is stuck servicing orders you already have, you won't have enough to invest in customers you don't yet have. Your business will always be stuck in the past, without the means to move into the future.

9. What is your profit rate?

How healthy is your bottom line?

The combination of 25% plus profits, with 90% recurring revenue, less than 5% churn, 90% gross margin and with plenty of liquidity validates your business model and sets up your business for generating even more value. In short, this is an extremely valuable organisation.

Build a business model that positions your firm for even greater value while demonstrating its current value. This sets you up for a healthy exit – and you will be in a position to determine both the timing and terms of that exit.

Initial Public Offering (IPO)

Once you have established a valuable organisation, you may want to consider an initial public offering (IPO). Jason Fernando describes an IPO as:

> offering shares of your private entity to the public in a new stock issuance. Public share issuance allows your organisation to raise capital from public investors. The transition from a private to a public company can be an important time for private investors to fully realise gains from their investment, as it typically includes share premiums for current private investors. Meanwhile, it also allows public investors to participate in the offering (Fernando, 2020).

IPOs can be used for various reasons, such as raising money to pay off debt, fund capital expenditure, or for growth. An IPO also creates exposure for your firm and may lead to growth in your market share. As a founder, you can also use an IPO to cash out – it could be your exit strategy. It is, however, not easy to run a listed entity. The standards for compliance and governance as well as financial reporting are high. It also comes with costs in being required to generate financial reporting documents. Audit fees need to be paid. There must be investor-relations departments, as well as accounting-oversight committees.

My advice is that even at inception you must understand what goes into running a listed entity. Within your means, try to uphold that standard from the get-go. Build muscle memory in your organisation in preparation for your exit – be it an IPO or selling to another firm. Maintaining the highest standards forces your business to make compliance governance a constant priority.

Design a gold-standard compliance-and-governance framework, instead of merely relying on the varied moral compasses of the employees and partners. As the founder and owner/CEO/MD, you must take a detailed, personal interest in all facets of your organisation – sales, marketing, finance, operations, human resources and technology, for instance. As much as you will hire people who are smarter than you in those areas, you must know more *about* those faculties than they do. You must get into the minutest, granular detail of the data and the levers that influence outputs and outcomes in those areas. Why? Because you are ultimately accountable. If non-compliance happens in any corner of your organisation, you don't have the excuse that you were unaware of it.

International Financial Reporting Standards (IFRS) has set standard rules so that financial statements are clear, consistent, transparent and comparable around the world. These financial reporting standards are issued by the International Accounting Standards Board (IASB). They outline exactly how organisations must manage and report their accounts, how they define types of transactions, as well as other events with financial impact.

Primarily, IFRSs were established to create a common accounting language so that businesses and their financial statements could be consistent and reliable across industries and countries. I would implore you to adopt IFRS at the outset – and don't simply leave it to the financial team to drive it. As business owner, you must be personally invested in the inner workings of IFRS and how your organisation adheres to them. A good exercise to do is to follow one rand in order to see how it flows through your organisation.

Selling your company

Another way to exit your organisation is to sell your company, or your stake in the company. What you, in fact, sell is equity in your firm, which is the value of your organisation minus liabilities it owes that are not transferrable with the sale. You can effectively prepare to sell your organisation from the moment you start it. This means that you will be prepared for this eventuality in terms of how your organisation is structured, your financial records, the customer base and what you'd like to sell the business for. A well-planned transition also helps the new owner/s baseline their start and grow from there.

Commission a business valuation through a third-party organisation. A business valuation determines the economic value of your organisation – how much it's worth. This will help you price your business accurately when pitching to potential buyers.

There are a few ways that your company can be valued.

The earnings multiplier uses the method of adjusting the future profits of your company against cashflow that could be invested at the current interest rate over the same period of time. In other words, it adjusts the current price-to-earnings (P/E) ratio to account for current interest rates. The P/E ratio is basically what investors are willing to pay for a rand worth of earnings. It is determined by dividing your company's share price by its earnings per share.

Another method is the discounted cashflow (DCF) method of business valuation, and it is similar to the earnings multiplier. DCF is primarily based on a forecast of future cashflows. These projections are then discounted to determine the current market value of the company.

There are a number of other business valuation methodologies, which can all help give you a rounded view of your organisation.

You will hear the term "multiple" a lot when you are selling or buying a company or a part of it. A valuation multiple is a financial measurement tool that evaluates one financial measure or metric as a ratio of another. This is handy when comparing different companies. It is based on the notion that similar assets should sell at similar prices. Research what multiples the businesses in your industry have sold for. This will be useful for benchmarking and during negotiations.

Consider using a broker, but stay involved and engage potential buyers personally. A broker will help with administration of the sale so you can keep looking after the business. They can also assist in achieving the highest possible price during the bidding process. Brokers always have an incentive to negotiate effectively, as their commission is based on price.

Your documentation must be prepared, going back at least five years – including audited annual financial statements, management accounts and financial projections. Prepare customer-base information and contract status – for example, how many annuity contracts your business has, as well as the terms of those contracts. As we said, your organisation becomes more valuable the more recurring business it has. Also create a list of assets and equipment to be sold. Include a valuation of any properties included in the sale. You must also prepare a business plan, as well as an operational manual detailing exactly how the business operates. Include the standards and operational certifications.

Finding a buyer is a complex process that takes an average of 18 months to conclude. Be sure to start the process with a non-disclosure agreement. To offset the risk of the one falling through, evaluate more than one potential buyer at a time. Find out whether the buyers will pay in cash or if they'll finance the purchase. If they're looking to finance, ask them to pre-qualify, which will expedite the process. If you're considering vendor-financing the transaction, you must work with an accountant and a lawyer. Ultimately, the purchase agreement comes with a guarantee of funds.

Liquidation

Another way to exit your business could be liquidation – in other words, you close the business down and sell its assets. Liquidation has negative connotations in that it's often associated with companies that are insolvent and cannot honour their obligations. However, there is no shame in liquidation, and you should consider it if you're struggling to sell at your ideal exit price. Perhaps your business is less than the sum of parts.

Ultimately, defining an exit strategy helps you outline the blueprint for your organisation's future. It informs the decisions you make and the tactics and structures you employ. It also helps you handle unsolicited offers. If you're clear what your exit looks like, you won't accept just any offer. It must align with your exit goals.

You will also know the value of your company. Being prepared will make your organisation more attractive to buyers. A clear exit strategy will also allow you to be vigilant and able to fight off hostile takeovers. Most importantly, you will know the right time to exit and which method or deal is best for you. Poetically, if you plan your exit, it will help to shape your life after the business.

12 Mindfulness

Entrepreneurship requires consistency, resilience, adaptability, mental strength and acute awareness. All of this must be rooted in mindfulness. Unfortunately, mindfulness is not something taught in business schools, and yet it is an essential element of success. The dictionary describes mindfulness as:

> a mental state achieved by focusing one's awareness on the present moment, while calmly acknowledging and accepting one's feelings, thoughts, and bodily sensations, used as a therapeutic technique (Lexico, 2020).

Mindfulness means to be fully present, to achieve complete focus on the task at hand. It's a useful trait for entrepreneurs, because we may otherwise be distracted by all the many moving parts. It is easy to drown in issues rather than focus on steering the business to success. A focused, present mind allows one to navigate challenges, focused on a single goal.

Failure is a part of success; you need to embrace it, and even get to the point where you appreciate it. When you can appreciate failure, you start to derive true value from it. Failure is merely course correction. It creates balance in that it offsets the grandeur of success with a degree of humility. For me it has been my greatest teacher. I see failure as a friend and companion, imparting the secrets of success. Every one of my accomplishments was preceded by failure. Over time, stumbling became the first sign that success was on its way. This taught me resilience, patience and adaptability.

Failure also taught me the power of letting go. I take nothing to heart or to mind. That goes for success and failure alike, even though I appreciate them as outcomes. I learn from them and try to use them for the greater good – teaching, mentoring and guiding anyone willing to learn. In my mentorship journey, I've found that my mentees actually learn more from my failures than from my successes. This is because failure is universal, but success is subjective.

To achieve the power of letting go, I first let go of trying to control the world around me. The second step was the realisation that the only thing I can control is myself – how I see the world and I how I engage with it. To me, this meant that if the world is tough, then I must be tougher. It meant that the four faculties I use to interface with the world must be at their sharpest at all times. These faculties are: a strong, sharp mind; a high emotional intelligence; a sound, connected spiritual vibration; and a fit body. When these faculties are primed, you can deal with all eventualities. Most importantly, by influencing how you react to eventualities, you can start to influence their outcomes. By doing this, you take back control. You stop being the victim of your circumstances, and become the master of your domain. By mastering yourself, you become the conductor of your circumstances. Things no longer happen to you – you happen to them.

People may use words, facial expressions and even body language to lie and gain your trust, but energy never lies. This is why it is said that you need to trust your instinct, or your gut feeling. It is your sense of the underlying energy.

Create a protective layer around your energy; consistently purify and recharge your energy through morning and evening meditation. Throughout the day, find five-minute slots to sit in the sun or a quiet space and breathe deeply, think of something beautiful, and clear your mind.

Use this control as your compass to navigate life, where your happiness is at the centre of everything. Aim for mind, body, spirit and emotional balance. This will inform your choices – for instance, whom you allow into your space, when, how and why. It will also inform what you do, with whom, when and how. Focus on things that charge your energy and passion, instead of those that drain it.

Being mindful helps reduce stress and enhance performance, while helping you make better decisions. Mindfulness can help you regulate your responses to situations by observing your own mind.

I also practise transcendental meditation. Otherwise known as TM, it focuses on a restful state of mind beyond thinking. What I enjoy most about it is that it's fairly easy to master. Transcendental meditation is not a religion or a philosophy, but a technique of tapping into our most relaxed mental states in order to reset and recharge the mind, body and spirit. This type of meditation is not one-size-fits-all. It involves finding out what works for you. As a result, anyone can do it – even if you think you can't meditate. TM does not require you to concentrate, filter out thoughts or suppress them. It's part of our nature that trying to do anything will present resisting thoughts. You end up with arguing notions. This can cause even more stress in some people. Rather, just let go. There are certified teachers who can train you in mastering authentic transcendental meditation techniques. Personally, I wake up at 4 am and meditate daily, followed by reading. I then plan the day ahead. This helps me reset and prepare to take on the new day with a fresh mindset, taking my learnings from the previous day into the new day. This allows me to take on each day on its own unique merit without drudging the challenges of the previous day. Each day is like opening a new gift with new opportunities to explore.

Decisions

The term "decision" has been used throughout this playbook – which speaks to the importance of great decision-making in life and in business. Sharpening the tools that help you make great decisions is paramount. A decision can be the difference between success and failure; life and death; or today and tomorrow. Good decision-making is therefore also a vital part of an organisation's success. It is a skill that you can master. Aaron De Smet and Gregor Jost write that there are keys to unlocking great decision-making:

> You can tell an organisation has problems making decisions when you hear these complaints: The organisation is "too complex", possesses a "meeting culture", or has "too much consensus". "Too complex" can simply be code for "it's too hard to get things done". And while people often finger too many "cooks" as the culprit, we've seen matrix structures where, despite many people being involved, roles are clear, how things work is straightforward, and decision-making is fast and effective (De Smet and Jost, 2018).

De Smet and Jost state that getting decision-making right is pivotal. They say research shows firms with high decision velocity and quality grow 2.5 times more. They also show double the profits and yield 30% more return on invested capital. The inverse of this is that when processes are not clearly defined, creating a "fog of accountability", where no one wants to take responsibility for anything. This creates corporate inertia, where people are running fast to remain in the very same position. Unfortunately, because time moves forward, they in fact move backwards. It's an environment of chronic indecision.

This is why you must marry empowerment with accountability. Each person empowered to make a decision must be accountable for all outcomes of that decision. The craft of making great decisions is often overlooked, but it must be defined. The people in your organisation must be pulling towards the same goals, using different vantage points, influenced by culture, guided by the values, steered by the mission and vision and driven by what connects them to the bigger goal.

For me, mindfulness has been valuable in leading high-performing teams. I am always mindful to remove "decision constipation" in an organisation by removing the fear of failure.

Mindfulness and business strategy may seem like polar opposites, because the former seems unstructured and the latter requires an organised approach. However, if they're applied in tandem, they can complement each other and yield positive results. I combine them by using the structure of strategy to produce results based on the notion that humanity must prevail in all that we do.

We must respect people from all walks of life, giving everyone the latitude to express themselves. The phrase "It's just business" is a poor excuse for treating people unfairly. We must be fair, just and kind at all times; we must aim for higher ideals. We must strive to be better than our best and do so responsibly. We must spread happiness, while living to fulfil our purpose.

To many organisations, these are fluffy ideals with no place in business strategy. To me, they are the outcomes business must aim for. Being mindful helps you see things as they are, and how to make them what they could, and should be.

Epilogue

The greatest ideas are generally extremely simple. So simple, in fact, that we often think, "Why didn't I think of that!" So many ideas seem so basic and obvious. There is beauty in that. Jazz pianist Charles Mingus once said, "Making the simple complicated is commonplace; making the complicated simple, awesomely simple … that's creativity."

On my journey, I have seen time and again how we bring complexity to things where there is none. This is why I say, "When you simplify how you understand your business, you simplify how customers see the value you offer." In this spirit, always try to keep things simple. Complexity tends to make things unnecessarily difficult. Simplicity brings ease. Since you will spend most of your time in business executing your idea, it makes sense to ease the process through simplicity. But be sure to execute.

Strike while the iron's hot

Ideas don't carry much value if they're not executed. They increase or even decrease in value once they have been implemented. This is why I advise young entrepreneurs to implement rather than spend lots of money on lawyers to protect an idea where the value is undetermined. If it is your idea, then position yourself to perform it better than anyone else can. This means establishing better competitive advantages and a better market.

The reality is that if the idea is easy to replicate, it will be copied. That's why your success depends on how well you execute your idea, not how much you pay your lawyers to protect it.

Deploy rapidly

Tech specialist Chintan Oza's article "Fail fast, fail often and fail forward" articulates things well when he says the best approach is to just launch. That puts you under launch pressure, but it also gives you the benefit of immediate customer feedback. This will help you iterate and refine your value proposition. Another advantage is that you will do it cost-effectively, and if it doesn't work, you can pivot. Or you could shut it down and head in a different direction altogether.

Oza adds that this approach helps your organisation avoid big failures whilst enhancing your rate of success. He outlines the following benefits of the "fail forward fast" approach, the same one outlined in the benefits of Rapid Deployment as defined in Chapter One:

- *Be agile* Being agile lets you execute rapidly, iterate and pivot quicker to a working solution.
- *Increase speed to market* Rapid deployment is a competitive advantage. Do not be afraid of the customer. Instead, partner with them to drive your success by fuelling theirs.
- *Save costs* By failing fast, failing often and failing forward,

you will avoid big, catastrophic failures. This will save you a lot of money.
- *Innovate* Rapid deployment allows you to try innovative ideas, and more of them. This would be too costly if done in an enormous "big-bang" approach.
- *Build innovation as culture* Rapid deployment creates a culture of iterative innovation and continuous improvement for your business.
- *Accelerate* By running minimum viable products or pilots, you can define the best customer approach. This will help you accelerate success.
- *Be resilient* Rapid deployment allows you to cultivate a steady roadmap of concepts and ideas, giving you options that will make your business more resilient to change.
- *Be adaptable to change* Your organisation's internal strengths will be able to adapt to the ever-changing external environment as you stay ahead of the change curves.
- *Get comfortable in uncertainty* Rapid deployment will equip your organisation to find strengths and opportunities even in uncertain times.
- *Have a higher tolerance for risk* The rapid deployment method increases your tolerance for risk by creating flexibility in your organisation.

Invest in yourself

No one will ever care more about your idea more than you do. It is also not their job to care. You will get help along the way, but you must invest yourself in your idea. Bringing it to life is entirely up to you. You should be mentally conditioned to carry it all the way through – on your own if you have to. Even when you have hired your first employees, they will not work as hard as you and you should not expect them to.

You need to be creative about raising funds to resource your firm. This must be a skill that you hone, because it's one you will need for the entire life of your business. For example, you could invest on the stock market to finance the development of your product or service. This is an approach I have used before to develop a product I knew would be hard to fund through traditional methods. It was a new project, and the business was a start-up with no history of trading. So the business didn't even have a balance sheet to fund against.

The product did not meet any of the funding parameters that traditional funders require. There were other options we could have explored but those would have meant we'd miss our proposed launch date.

With our investment, we had the fortune of great timing of a new IPO on the stock exchange, buying at the opening price and selling a week later at a high. I must declare that I am no expert in this field. I merely saw it as a means to an end, but I had done enough research and practice with small amounts, so I was comfortable with taking this calculated risk. I started by reading everything I could find on the impending IPO. At the same time, I began scraping together money from all of my savings accounts. I borrowed from my pension fund. By the time the stock listed, I had just about enough money to make a decent return should the stock close at a higher price per share (PPS) than the opening price. The risk was that I stood to lose a lot if the share closed lower than the opening price and did not recover. Fortunately for us, the stock increased by 63.8% post listing. This meant we made just about enough money to finance the product and it gave us a three-month runway.

I still had to find money for the all-important marketing of the product before, during and after the launch. It was a subscription-based product, so we approached our first customers and offered them a four-month discount on a 24-month contract if they could pay us cash upfront for the 20 months. We then used those funds to market the product. We established a base and focused on growing it. When you reach this stage, you have most funding options available to you, since you have shown that you have a viable product, a feasible and profitable business model, a market and customers.

Since this is your idea, you will need to invest your own time, money, commitment and creativity to bring it to life. Work to find the speediest route to your first sale, then sell, sell, sell! The best way to finance your endeavour is through actual sales.

Sell at the speed of currency

I used to drive long distances to find customers in far-flung small towns, figuring we wouldn't have much competition in these areas for our project management services. But I was wrong – there was plenty of competition!

I recall walking into a company I was hoping to provide services for in this beautiful, seemingly sleepy but cash-rich coastal town – one of those towns that does all right from tourism during the peak seasons. One hospital, three doctors … but enough retail to service the surrounding areas. These sort of towns generate a lot of cash, because you will find they are often the biggest retail and commercial precinct across an expansive district. The people it serves includes those in rural and township areas, and a smaller percentage of urbanites. Most of these people use cash.

So I sat down for an impromptu meeting with the owner of a local cleaning products manufacturer, who told me they had five companies they procured project management services from. He explained to me that they chose based on who had the best price each time they needed to use the services. What I also learned during this chat is that this company was a part of a network of local companies that would pool procurement so that they could get savings by buying at scale.

I knew at that moment that we needed to be among the companies they bought from, but that we had to set ourselves apart. I asked for a chance to do a small piece of work so that we were able to prove our ability. When we were granted that opportunity, we delivered with higher quality and greater speed than any of the other five companies. The other companies would take an average of a month to turn around a small project, but because we were trying to impress, we delivered a high-quality project in seven days. The customer had never seen such a quick turnaround, nor one of such quality.

We soon took over the full account and edged out the competition. None of them could match our speed and quality. If they had tried to, it would have cost them a lot of money and eaten into their profits. We had essentially locked them out of the account. We monopolised the problem we were solving. Word quickly spread around to the network and we started winning all of their project work as well. But then a new business problem emerged for us … Demand started to exceed our capacity.

Run fast

It was at this point that we realised it was time to enhance the business for optimal operations and success. We had to build scale. We viewed the pipeline of work as unbanked revenue. This meant there was a step we had to complete in order to unlock that revenue. We decided to conduct a scale-up exercise.

We used Rapid Replication and Proliferation, which involved finding out what did not work for us and then rapidly discarding it. This was so we could focus on what worked. Running fast meant we grew proportionally in scale and revenue. We built a stronger relationship with customers by continuing to deliver superior service faster.

Run faster

Because we had built scale, we now needed even more customers to justify the resources to support that scale. We did not want to be in a situation where it was costing us a fortune to deliver the services. This would put pressure on our margins and push our price up beyond what our market could afford. We had to establish our competitive advantages in order to enhance our chances of success against the competition and acquire more customers. More customers would also lower our cost of servicing them.

We had established that our quality was good and our speed of execution was great. But that comes at a cost, and the customer must be willing to pay for that. This is where we learned that not all customers prioritise the same things. Some customers were sensitive to price and thought they could compromise on quality and speed. To accommodate them – so they could still get the benefit of good quality delivered at speed – we changed our model. Where, before, we would invoice a project based on effort, complexity and time, we changed to a contract retainer model.

This meant we could dedicate resources by project, further enhancing our customer experience and speed, but allowing clients to pay smaller amounts, regularly, over longer periods. This solved something for us as a business. We had now moved to a 90% annuity model and only 10% of our revenue came from cash-upfront projects. This had various benefits – greater customer stickiness, security and a healthier balance sheet to help fund our growth. Most importantly, we improved our operating model so we were able to sell and serve at the speed of currency. This fuelled our growth.

Grow by solving for X and defining your formula of success

The science of business growth continues to amaze me. There are answers to all questions a business can ask. For instance, how do you grow a non-selling product, business segment or organisation? The answer is that you need a great plan, and even greater execution. The type that needs you to be hands on and detail driven. You also need a bit of time, and then you're on your way. This is an area I have come to specialise in, having done similar projects for international organisations as well as local ones.

I start by looking at the problem we are trying to solve for and the goals we are trying to achieve. I call this "Solving for X". Then I work backwards to define the formula of success that will ensure we get there. This is the plan. Then the all-important execution phase will immediately tell us if we have a good plan or not. The execution phase takes a plethora of tools to reach success – and an ability to adapt without losing focus on X.

I remember once taking over a product that was not selling well. It was a great product, but there were a couple of issues. The name of the product was odd; the operating model was broken; the go-to-market model was flawed; there was no marketing; and the product was not even clearly defined. But the market opportunity was certainly there!

First, we all aligned on what success would look like. We then set out to answer the following questions:

WHY: Why do we do what we do?
- Who is our customer?
- What do they need?
- Why do they need/want it?
- What are they willing to pay for it?
- How and where do they want it?
- When do they want it?

- What customers do we already have?
- What existing customers do we want to keep?
- Which new customers do we want?
- What does the customer we want look like in two, five, and 10 years' time?

HOW: How do we do what we do?
- What are our core competencies?
- What are our competitive advantages?
- What other competencies should we build?
- What other competitive advantages should we establish?
- Will our core established competencies and competitive advantages stand the test of time?

WHAT: What is it that we actually do?

Our formula of success became clearer once we had factually and honestly answered these questions. All we had to do was diligently execute against that formula of success. The result was that the product ended up becoming one of the biggest sellers in the business.

Create an ecosystem of success

American football coach Vince Lombardi once said, "Once you agree upon the price you and your family must pay for success, it enables you to ignore the minor hurts, the opponent's pressure, and the temporary failures."

It will help you to know that failure is an important part of success. If you can absorb the perils of failure and learn from them, then success is all but guaranteed.

In business, look to combine the following elements to enhance your chances of success and growth. Create an ecosystem that will support your endeavours. Within that ecosystem, make sure you have access to information, using data and insights to enhance and focus decision-making in your organisation. A second component of the ecosystem is skills. Tap into the appropriate talent, education and training to ensure your capabilities keep up with the evolving needs of your customers. The third element is access to technology. Technology is no longer an afterthought or a grudge purchase; used correctly, it is a competitive advantage.

In our digital economy, the entities that do not embrace technology will be left behind. Therefore, harness the limitless power of technology to propel your organisation to success. Just look at how the top five businesses in the world are using technology.

The fourth part of your business ecosystem is creating a partner network that complements your organisation, supplements your strengths and helps you attain your goals. The fifth element is an extremely rewarding one – customers who are willing to provide honest feedback. Creating a community of customers where dialogue thrives will help you co-create your value proposition, and define what matters to them and how they'd like to receive it.

The sixth component is finance. This is both a skill that you must develop and a facility you need to access. Finance – and your ability to raise funds – will serve you well at all stages of your business. It is something you will always need. It is a skill you can use to grow your firm to the point where it generates cash, becomes self-funding and is sustainable.

Exit

Determine your exit strategy at the outset and work hard to exit on your own terms. Give yourself permission to enjoy the fruits of your labour.

Mindfulness

Use mindfulness to mind your business.

The Young Entrepreneur's Playbook: Using failure as a shortcut to success

Success becomes a habit – as much as failure can be a habit, if it's not used to fuel success. I continue to apply this playbook daily in my work helping businesses grow. I am certain I will continue to learn; learning in business is a perpetual undertaking and I encourage you to embrace that.

At the time of publishing, we are launching Eden, the new digital platform to help enable entrepreneurs manage and grow their organisations.

This is where my passions have brought me. My advice is to find out where *your* passion and purpose collide – then set up permanent residence there. That's where you will find happiness and fulfilment, while making an impact greater than yourself. Strive for excellence, because that is the difference maker. It's undeniable.

Let's sum up! The basic steps of using your failure as a short cut to success are as follows:

Firstly, define and clarify your vision.

Secondly, you get to define your own formula of success. Trust your instincts and have confidence in the process of execution. Exist in the detail and execute against short timeframes and small milestones. They lead to big outcomes.

Thirdly, outline your exit strategy. This will be the GPS that guides you to your destination.

The fourth step is to visualise the outcome you desire and create the perception that you have already accomplished it. Then work very hard to actualise and maintain it.

The fifth step is assembling your dream team to bring your dream alive. This is why your vision must be clear – so you can easily explain to people, and have them come along with you.

The sixth step is that you must pay yourself. Never overlook this. Rewarding yourself for your efforts incentivises the hard work and the value you provide. You don't want to accept, even subconsciously, that it is all right to work without reward. This may create a habit and habits tend to invent reality.

Lastly, you need to execute for exponential growth, using failure as a shortcut to success. This means you must start, fail, learn, succeed and repeat at scale. The principle is that if you can sell to one customer, you can sell to a thousand. And if you can sell to a thousand, you can sell to a million. The limit is up to you. Try to be a servant leader; realise that you work for your customers and the teams that you lead towards that pursuit.

Of course, none of this is easy. If it were, everyone would be successful. This is simply a way to define your own formula of success. You still have to put in the hard work. All the best!

For my son

If—

RUDYARD KIPLING

If you can keep your head when all about you
Are losing theirs and blaming it on you,
If you can trust yourself when all men doubt you,
But make allowance for their doubting too;
If you can wait and not be tired by waiting,
Or being lied about, don't deal in lies,
Or being hated, don't give way to hating,
And yet don't look too good, nor talk too wise:

If you can dream – and not make dreams your master;
If you can think – and not make thoughts your aim;
If you can meet with Triumph and Disaster
And treat those two impostors just the same;
If you can bear to hear the truth you've spoken
Twisted by knaves to make a trap for fools,
Or watch the things you gave your life to, broken,
And stoop and build 'em up with worn-out tools:

If you can make one heap of all your winnings
And risk it on one turn of pitch-and-toss,
And lose, and start again at your beginnings
And never breathe a word about your loss;

Lindile Xoko

If you can force your heart and nerve and sinew
To serve your turn long after they are gone,
And so hold on when there is nothing in you
Except the Will which says to them: 'Hold on!'

If you can talk with crowds and keep your virtue,
Or walk with Kings – nor lose the common touch,
If neither foes nor loving friends can hurt you,
If all men count with you, but none too much;
If you can fill the unforgiving minute
With sixty seconds' worth of distance run,
Yours is the Earth and everything that's in it,
And – which is more – you'll be a Man, my son!

Bibliography

Accenture, 2016. 'A $12 billion opportunity for South Africa: Harnessing the power of open innovation through digital collaboration'. Available at: https://www.accenture.com/_acnmedia/PDF-28/Accenture-Harnessing-Power-Entrepreneurs-Open-Innovation-South-Africa.pdf (accessed 14 February 2021).

Agina, W., Ahlback, K., De Smet, A., Lackey, G., Lurie, M., Murarka, M. and Handscomb, C., 2018. 'The five trademarks of agile organizations'. Available at: https://www.mckinsey.com/business-functions/organization/our-insights/the-five-trademarks-of-agile-organization (accessed 14 February 2021).

Airbnb Newsroom, 2019. 'About us – Airbnb Newsroom'. Available at: https://news.airbnb.com/about-us/ (accessed 14 February 2021).

Airfocus.com, 2021. 'What is a go-to-marketsStrategy? Go-to-market strategy definition, components, & FAQ'. Available at: https://airfocus.com/glossary/what-is-a-go-to-market-strategy/ (accessed 14 February 2021).

Am, J., Furstenthal, L., Jorge, F. and Roth, E., 2020. 'Prioritizing innovation today is the key to unlocking postcrisis growth – Innovation in a crisis: Why it is more critical than ever'. Available at: https://www.mckinsey.com/~/media/McKinsey/Business%20Functions/Strategy%20and%20Corporate%20Finance/Our%20Insights/Innovation%20in%20a%20crisis%20Why%20it%20is%20more%20critical%20than%20ever/Innovation-in-a-crisis-Why-it-is-more-critical-than-ever-vF.pdf (accessed 14 February 2021).

Backstrom, T., 2009. 'How to organize for local resource generation'. *The Learning Organization*, 16(3): 223–236.

Balogun, J. and Hope Hailey, V., 2004. *Exploring Strategic Change*, 1st ed. Harlow: Prentice Hall/*Financial Times*.

Banton, C., 2020. 'The definition of efficiency'. Available at: https://www.investopedia.com/terms/e/efficiency.asp (accessed 14 February 2021).

Bennet, A. and Bennet, D., 2003. 'Designing the knowledge organization of the future: The intelligent complex adaptive system', in Holsapple C.W. (ed), *Handbook on Knowledge Management*. International Handbooks on Information Systems, vol. 2, pp. 623–638.

Brown, M., 2017. '12 signs your business model may be broken'. Available at: https://www.bizcommunity.com/Article/196/610/162129.html (accessed 14 February 2021).

Bujak, J.S., 1999. 'Culture in chaos: The need for leadership and followership in medicine'. *Physician Exec*, 25(3): 17–24.

Business Insider, 2021. 'Airbnb worth more than 3 hotel giants combined after its stock popped 143% on first trading day'. Available at: https://www.businessinsider.co.za/airbnb-ipo-valuation-tops-three-hotel-chains-combined-opening-day-2020-12?r=US&IR=T (accessed 14 February 2021).

Cisco, A. and Office, C., 2020. 'Acquisitions'. Available at: https://www.cisco.com/c/en/us/about/corporate-strategy-office/acquisitions.html (accessed 14 February 2021).

Cohen, P. and Tedesco, L., 2009. 'Willing, ready, and able? How we must exercise leadership for needed change in dental education'. *Journal of Dental Education*, 73(1): 3–11.

Crawford, C., 2020. 'Examples of business competency'. Available at: https://yourbusiness.azcentral.com/examples-business-competency-9072.html (accessed 14 February 2021).

Culture Amp Blog, 2021. \How Airbnb is building its culture through belonging'. Available at: https://www.cultureamp.com/blog/how-airbnb-is-building-its-culture-through-belonging/ (accessed 14 February 2021).

Dalgård, T. and Jørgensen, E., 2016. 'Four dogmas for creating powerful competency models'. Available at: https://implementconsultinggroup.com/four-dogmas-for-creating-powerful-competency-models/ (accessed 14 February 2021).

De Smet, A. and Jost, G., 2018. 'Keys to unlocking great decision-making'. Available at: https://www.mckinsey.com/business-functions/organization/our-insights/the-organization-blog/keys-to-unlocking-great-decision-making (accessed 14 February 2021).

Deloitte Consulting, 2013. *2013 Global Contact Center Survey*. Available at: https://www2.deloitte.com/us/en/pages/operations/articles/2013-global-contact-center-survey.html (accessed 14 February 2021).

Deloitte, 2013. 'We're just getting started: The analytics advantage'. Available at: https://www2.deloitte.com/content/dam/Deloitte/global/Documents/Deloitte-Analytics/dttl-analytics-analytics-advantage-report-061913.pdf (accessed 14 February 2021).

Fenwick, T., 2010. 'Response to Jeffrey McClellan: Complexity theory, leadership, and the traps of Utopia'. *Complicity: An International Journal of Complexity and Education*, 7(2).

Fernando, J., 2020. 'Initial public offering (IPO)'. Available at: https://www.investopedia.com/terms/i/ipo.asp (accessed 14 February 2021).

Fernando, J., 2021. 'Understanding cost of goods sold – COGS'. Available at: https://www.investopedia.com/terms/c/cogs.asp (accessed 14 February 2021).

Folkman, J., 2016. '5 ways to build a high-performance team'. Available at: https://www.forbes.com/sites/joefolkman/2016/04/13/are-you-on-the-team-from-hell-5-ways-to-create-a-high-performance-team/?sh=7f7d08df7ee2 (accessed 14 February 2021).

Gavin, M., 2019. 'Business analytics: What it is and why it's important'. *Business Insights* (Blog). Available at: https://online.hbs.edu/blog/post/importance-of-business-analytics (accessed 14 February 2021).

Gudehus-Wittern, G., 2017. 'If you want real relationships with your customers, start being a better partner'. Available at: https://www.entrepreneur.com/article/295952 (accessed 14 February 2021).

Hatch, J. and Zwaig, J., 2001. 'Strategic flexibility: The key to growth'. *Ivey Business Journal*. Available at: https //iveybusinessjournal.com/publication/strategic-flexibility-the-key-to-growth/ (accessed 14 February 2021).

Hayes, A., 2020. 'Learn about elasticity'. Available at: https://www.investopedia.com/terms/e/elasticity.asp (accessed 14 February 2021).

Henderson, T., 2017. 'Council post: Why innovation is crucial to your organization's long-term success'. *Forbes*. Available at: <https://www.forbes.com/sites/forbescoachescouncil/2017/05/08/why-innovation-is-crucial-to-your-organizations-long-term-success/?sh=5362109a3098 (accessed 14 February 2021).

Hilburt-Davis, J., 2000. 'Learning from complexity theory: Is strategic planning obsolete?'. (Practice Paper) The Family Firm Institute, Inc. Lexington.

Impraise, 2021. 'What is psychological safety and why is it the key to great teamwork?'. Available at: https://www.impraise.com/blog/what-is-psychological-safety-and-why-is-it-the-key-to-great-teamwork (accessed 14 February 2021).

Jakes, T., 2017. Twitter post. Available at: https://twitter.com/bishopjakes/status/821688845972414464?lang=en (accessed 14 February 2021).

Jobs, S., 1997. 'The iconic think different. Apple commercial narrated by Steve Jobs. (Blog). Available at: https://fs.blog/2016/03/steve-jobs-crazy-ones/ (accessed 14 February 2021).

Jobs, S., 2020. 'The rumors – and truth – behind Steve Jobs's last words'. *Reader's Digest*. Available at: https://www.rd.com/article/the-rumors-and-truth-behind-steve-jobs-last-words/ (accessed 14 February 2021).

Johnson, G., Scholes, K., Johnson, G. and Whittington, R., 2011. *Exploring Strategy*, 1st ed. Harlow: Prentice Hall/*Financial Times*.

Kark, K., Briggs, B. and Tweardy, J., 2021. 'Reimagining the role of technology'. *CIO Insider*. Available at: https://www2.deloitte.com/us/en/insights/focus/cio-insider-business-insights/reimagining-role-of-technology-business-strategies.html (accessed 14 February 2021).

Kipling, R., 1910. *Rewards and Fairies*. London: Macmillan.

Kravitz, D. and Martin, B., 1986. 'Ringelmann rediscovered: The original article'. *Journal of Personality and Social Psychology*, 50(5): 936–941.

LaBerge, L., O'Toole, C., Schneider, J. and Smaje, K., 2020. 'How COVID-19 has pushed companies over the technology tipping point – and transformed business forever'. McKinsey & Co. Available at: https://www.mckinsey.com/business-functions/strategy-and-corporate-finance/our-insights/how-covid-19-has-pushed-companies-over-the-technology-tipping-point-and-transformed-business-forever (accessed 14 February 2021).

Lexico Dictionaries: English, 2020. 'Mindfulness'. Available at: https://www.lexico.com/definition/mindfulness (accessed 14 February 2021).

Lotz, S., Raabe, J. and Roggenhofer, S., 2018. 'The role of customer care in a customer experience transformation'. McKinsey & Co. Available at: https://www.mckinsey.com/~/media/McKinsey/Business%20Functions/Operations/Our%20Insights/The%20role%20of%20customer%20care%20in%20a%20customer%20experience%20transformation/The-role-of-customer-care-in-a-customer-experience-transformation-vf.pdf (accessed 14 February 2021).

Medium, 2021. 'The richest place on earth'. Available at: https://medium.com/@kevin_chung/the-richest-place-on-earth-41823f5065 (accessed 14 February 2021).

Michigan State University, 2019. Available at: https://www.michiganstateuniversityonline.com/resources/leadership/qualities-of-effective-change-agents/ (accessed 14 February 2021).

Moore, K., 2015. 'The great power of connecting passion with purpose'. *Forbes*. Available at: https://www.forbes.com/sites/karlmoore/2015/01/19/the-great-power-of-connecting-passion-with-purpose/?sh=5e713d478784 (accessed 14 February 2021).

OECD, 2021. 'Development finance institutions and private sector development'. Available at: https://www.oecd.org/development/development-finance-institutions-private-sector-development.htm (accessed 14 February 2021).

Oza, C., 2017. 'Fail fast, fail often, fail forward is the answer to enhance rate of success!'. *LinkedIn* Available at: https://www.linkedin.com/pulse/yes-fail-fast-oftenfail-forward-answer-enhance-rate-success-oza/ (accessed 14 February 2021).

Palmer, B., 2020. 'International Financial Reporting Standards (IFRS)'. *Investopedia*. Available at: https://www.investopedia.com/terms/i/ifrs.asp (accessed 14 February 2021).

Porter, M. and Kramer, M., 2011. *Creating Shared Value*. Boston, MA: Harvard University, Graduate School of Business Administration.

Porter, M., 1996. 'What is strategy?'. *Harvard Business Review*. Available at: https://hbr.org/1996/11/what-is-strategy> (accessed 14 February 2021).

Power, R., 2020. '4 ways to build a successful partnership'. Available at: https://www.inc.com/rhett-power/4-ways-to-build-a-successful-partnership.html (accessed 14 February 2021)

Qualaroo, 2020. 'The ultimate customer journey map template (and guide)'. Available at: https://qualaroo.com/customer-journey-map-template/ (accessed 14 February 2021).

Roberts, S., 2020. '3 buyer persona examples'. Cyberclick.net. Available at: https://www.cyberclick.net/numericalblogen/3-buyer-persona-examples (accessed 14 February 2021).

Schleckser, J., 2020. 'These 9 questions will tell you if you have a great business model'. Inc.com. Available at: https://www.inc.com/jim-schleckser/these-nine-questions-will-tell-you-if-you-have-a-great-business-model.html (accessed 14 February 2021).

Silverthorne, C. and Wang, T., 2001. 'Situational leadership style as a predictor of success and productivity among Taiwanese business organizations'. *The Journal of Psychology*, 135(4): 399–412.

Simons, R., 1994. 'Control in an age of empowerment'. *Harvard Business Review*. Available at: https://hbr.org/1995/03/control-in-an-age-of-empowerment (accessed 14 February 2021).

Sinek, S., 2011. *Start with Why*. London: Penguin Books.

Smith, R., 2020. 'Explaining the VRIO framework (with a real-life example)'. ClearPoint Strategy. Available at: https://www.clearpointstrategy.com/vrio-framework/ (accessed 14 February 2021).

Smith, T., 2020. 'Crowdfunding. Hampton Roads Innovative Collaborative'. Available at: https://technologyhamptonroads.com/crowdfunding/ (accessed 14 February 2021).

Tardi, C., 2020. 'What is a value chain?' *Investopedia*. Available at: https://www.investopedia.com/terms/v/valuechain.asp (accessed 14 February 2021).

The Institute of You, 2021. 'Mindfulness for you'. Available at: https://instituteofyou.org/ (accessed 7 April 2021).

Tobias, A., 1983. *Fire and Ice*. New York, NY: Quill.

Tredgold, G., 2020. '4 reasons Why You Need To Focus On Innovation. Inc.com. Available at: https://www.inc.com/gordon-tredgold/4-reasons-why-you-need-to-focus-on-innovation.html (accessed 14 February 2021).

Twin, A., 2020. 'Competitive advantage: What gives companies an edge'. *Investopedia*. Available at: https://www.investopedia.com/terms/c/competitive_advantage.asp (accessed 14 February 2021).

Amazon, 2020. 'Our mission'. Available at: https://www.aboutamazon.co.uk/uk-investment/our-mission (accessed 14 February 2021).

Vessel, B., 2021. 'Customer journey map example: Use to define your customer experience'. Available at: https://www.brightvessel.com/customer-journey-map-2018/ (accessed 10 July 2021).

Welch, J. and Welch, S, 2006. *Winning*. New York: Collins.

Wertz, J., 2018. 'Why instant gratification is the one marketing tactic companies should focus on right now'. *Forbes*. Available at: https://www.forbes.com/sites/jiawertz/2018/04/30/why-instant-gratification-is-the-one-marketing-tactic-companies-should-focus-on-right-now/?sh=1ecec302e91b (accessed 14 February 2021).

White, L., 2019. 'Amazon VRIO analysis: Competitive advantages, core competencies'. Rancord Society. Available at: https://www.rancord.org/amazon-vrio-analysis-competitive-advantages-core-competencies (accessed 14 February 2021).

Worldometer, 2021. 'Real time world statistics'. Available at: https://www.worldometers.info (accessed 14 February 2021).

Writer, S., 2020. 'Food delivery in South Africa is huge: The crazy numbers behind Mr D Food'. BusinessTech. Available at: https://businesstech.co.za/news/mobile/360068/food-delivery-in-south-africa-is-huge-the-crazy-numbers-behind-mr-d-food/ (accessed 14 February 2021).

Xoko, L., 2021. 'Eden – myBusinessUniverse'. Edenonline. Available at: https://edenonline.biz (accessed 14 February 2021).